CAMPFIRE TALES OF JACKSON HOLE

Edited by Merlin K. Potts
Former Chief Naturalist, Grand Teton National Park

Illustrated by Ruth Harmon

GRAND TETON NATURAL HISTORY ASSOCIATION
GRAND TETON NATIONAL PARK
MOOSE, WYOMING

Acknowledgements

"The Story of Deadman's Bar" was reprinted from Annals of Wyoming, Volume 5, Number 4, June 1929, with permission from the author and Miss Lola M. Homsher, Director of Archives and Historical Department, State of Wyoming.

"The Affair at Cunningham's Ranch" was reprinted from *Saga*, literary magazine of Augustana College, 1955, with permission of the author and the editor of *Saga*.

"Prospector of Jackson Hole" was reprinted from *American Forests*, October 1935, with permission of the author and editor of *American Forests*.

"Mountain River Men" was reprinted from the *Empire Magazine* of *The Denver Post* and from the *Jackson's Hole Courier* with permission of the editors and the author.

Published in 1960. Revised Edition, 1990. Reprinted 2004.

Project Coordinator: Sharlene Milligan
Book Design: Lee Riddell (cover), Jackie Gilmore (inside pages)
Printing: Patterson Printing, Benton Harbor, MI

ISBN 0-931895-12-X

CONTENTS

FOREWORD

The Grand Teton Natural History Association takes pleasure in making available this booklet which is devoted to a few of the fascinating historical tales of the Jackson Hole country. Here, for the first time, have been gathered together these stories of the colorful past of the region—a past rich in the folklore and romance of the West.

Here, too, for the first time, is a source booklet of stories suitable for telling in the magic, flickering light of the campfire. These are tales which have been told around the campfires in Jackson Hole. They are a partial basis for understanding the history of the region.

On every hand there is interest in history. There is an ever-increasing attention to the American background in history and folklore. A great many of the interesting stories of the Jackson Hole region have been lost, but some have survived. A few have come down to us by word of mouth from old timers; others have come from official reports, some from the press, from diaries and from old letters.

That these tales of the past are available is remarkable. Few of the mountain men, trappers, prospectors and wanderers who came into the country in the early 1800s were inclined to write very much. Indeed, they were occupied with the important task of preserving life and limb a great deal of the time.

The references used in preparing the articles which deal with the period of the Western Fur Trade will provide hours of entertainment for the reader who may wish to pursue the subject further. No other era in America's past has captured the fancy and imagination of our people quite so well.

I hope you find *Campfire Tales* a valuable aid in enhancing your interest and knowledge of the human history of this region.

HARTHON L. BILL, Superintendent
Grand Teton National Park
1960

R. HARMON

JOHN COLTER

THE DISCOVERY OF JACKSON HOLE AND THE YELLOWSTONE

by Merlin K. Potts

To John Colter, mountain man, trapper, and lone wanderer in the exploration of the Rocky Mountain wilderness, belongs the distinction of being the first white man to enter Jackson Hole and the "Country of the Yellowstone."

His biographers record that Colter was a descendant of Micajah Coalter, Scotsman, who settled in Virginia about 1700. That John was born in Virginia is not definitely known, but there is no evidence to indicate that any of the Coalters, from John's great-great-grandfather to his own generation, ever lived elsewhere. He was born toward the close of the eighteenth century, probably about 1775. There are no records of Colter's early life, other than to indicate emigration to Kentucky with other members of the family, before 1803. History marks his first appearance with his enlistment in the Lewis and Clark Expedition of October 15 of that year. He proved to be a skillful hunter, a faithful and reliable employee, popular with his commanders and the other men of the expedition. He served with Lewis and Clark on the westward journey and was returning to St. Louis in August 1806, when the party, commanded by Captain Clark, encountered two trappers en route to a winter's sojourn on the upper Missouri. Colter expressed a desire to join these men and was released from the expedition to do so. The partnership dissolved in the spring of 1807, after what appears to have been an unsuccessful venture insofar as peltry was concerned, but undoubtedly rewarding, experience-wise.

Colter again started for St. Louis by canoe down the Missouri. By now he was an experienced hand in unknown country. Moving alone and matching his skills against the hazards and rigors of the land were no more than everyday occurrences. As he swept down the turbid river swollen by spring flood water, his intention was to return to the civilization he had left three years before. Once again his plans were altered by chance.

A young Spaniard, Manuel Lisa, engaged in the fur trade in St. Louis and influenced by reports of the abundance of beaver on the upper Missouri, had determined to explore the possibilities of extending his operations in that hitherto unexploited region. Accordingly, he organized a brigade and set forth up river. Colter met the party and was persuaded by Lisa to join him. Lisa, a shrewd trader, was not a frontiersman. He recognized in Colter exactly the type of man he needed, and quite probably the inducements he offered were considerable. Yet, to a man of Colter's stamp, the financial gain possible was secondary to the prospect of further opportunity for adventure. We can surmise that Lisa experienced little difficulty in influencing the young and venturesome trapper to turn his back again on the doubtful attractions of the settlements.

It was late in November of that year, 1807, before Lisa selected a site for his trading post at the confluence of the Yellowstone and Big Horn rivers in what is now south-central Montana. Construction of the post was begun immediately. Lisa named it Fort Raymond after his son, but it was more generally known as Manuel's Fort.

It was Lisa's objective not only to trap, but to engage in trade with the Indians and to learn as much as possible about the trapping territory to the west. Of his men, Colter was the best suited to seek out the tribesmen, encourage them to trade at the post, and survey the lands with an eye to its productivity in fur. Thus Lisa instructed him, outfitted him, and sent him forth.

It could not have been earlier than late November when Colter set out. His equipment must have been meager: snowshoes, his gun, ammunition, a blanket or robe, and little or no food, since he would have intended to "live off the land," and his pack would likely not have exceeded thirty pounds, including "geegaws" for the Indians he encountered.

His exact route has long been a matter for conjecture among historians. He was to venture into country unknown to any other than the Indians, he carried no maps, and he followed what must have appeared to him to be the route of least resistance, insofar as he could judge the terrain he traversed. He, from force of circumstance, must have followed the watercourses and game trails and sought the lowest mountain passes he could find, pursuing a devious course which led him to the south and west.

In the light of Colter's own later attempt to trace his route for Captain Clark, and through our knowledge of today's maps, it can be assumed with a fair degree of reliability that he moved across country to Pryor's Fork, up that stream and down Gap Creek to its junction with the Bighorn, thence up the Bighorn to the Shoshone (Stinking Water). He followed the course of the Shoshone upstream to the vicinity of what is now Cody, Wyoming, and along the base of the Absaroka Mountains into the Wind River Valley, striking the Wind probably some distance south and east of present-day Dubois.

It appears that it was on the Stinking Water that Colter discovered the area which his contemporaries of the trapping fraternity derisively named "Colter's Hell" after Colter's description of the thermal features there. Historians writing many years later, perhaps more romantically than accurately, attributed Colter's reference to one or more of the now famous geyser and hot springs sections of the Yellowstone. It makes a better story thus, but the preponderance of evidence from the accounts of the trappers themselves places "Colter's Hell" in the vicinity of the DeMaris Springs, near Cody. Geological indications are that the area was much more active, insofar as thermal phenomena are concerned, then than now.

Two excellent early authorities confirm this location of "Colter's Hell." As set forth in Burton Harris's *John Colter, His Years in the Rockies:*

> As late as 1848, the accomplished Belgian priest, Father DeSmet, placed Colter's Hell on the Stinking Water on the strength of information obtained from the few trappers who were left in the mountains at that date. The courageous priest, known

as "Black Robe" to the Indians, was on his way to visit the Sioux in 1848 when he wrote the following account: "Near the source of the River Puante [Stinking Water, now called Shoshone] which empties into the Big Horn, and the sulphurous waters of which have probably the same medicinal qualities as the celebrated Blue Lick Springs of Kentucky, is a place called Colter's Hell—from a beaver hunter of that name. This locality is often agitated with subterranean fires. The sulphurous gases which escape in great volumes from the burning soil infect the atmosphere for several miles, and render the earth so barren that even the wild wormwood cannot grow on it. The beaver hunters have assured me that the frequent undergound noises and explosions are frightful."

Washington Irving in *The Rocky Mountains* (1837) says:

The Crow country has other natural curiosities, which are held in superstitious awe by the Indians, and considered great marvels by the trappers. Such is the Burning Mountain on Powder River, abounding with anthracite coal. Here the earth is hot and cracked; in many places emitting smoke and sulphurous vapors, as if covering concealed fires. A volcanic tract of similar character is found on Stinking River, one of the tributaries of the Big Horn, which takes its unhappy name from the odor derived from sulphurous springs and streams. This last mentioned place was first discovered by Colter, a hunter belonging to Lewis and Clark's exploring party, who came upon it in the course of his lonely wanderings, and gave such an account of its gloomy terrors, its hidden fires, smoking pits, noxious streams, and the all-pervading "smell of brimstone," that it received, and has ever since retained among the trappers, the name of "Colter's Hell!"

Upon reaching the valley of the Wind, it would have been logical for Colter's route to have been north and west over the Wind River Mountains through Union Pass, the easiest available, at an elevation of 9,210 feet. Here historians have indulged in a long standing and unresolvable debate, some authorities contending that he would probably have followed up the Little Wind River, crossing the Wind River Mountains further north, at Togwotee Pass. Whichever route he used to the westward—Union Pass and the Gros Ventre River drainage, or Togwotee Pass and Blackrock Creek—either brought him into Jackson Hole.

There can be little doubt that in any event his course was a circuitous one, following the twistings and turnings of many water courses, deviating along Indian trails to the winter encampments of the Crows and attentive to his instructions from Manuel Lisa. Quite probably the friendly Crows aided Colter by directing him to routes of easy passage, perhaps accompanying him over parts of his journey, though history makes no mention of this.

Entering Jackson Hole on its eastern margin, Colter saw before him a scene of unsurpassed grandeur. At this season, which must have been well into December, the floor of the Hole presented a broad expanse of snow-blanketed valley, broken only by the forested buttes looming black against the glistening white and the timbered water courses marked by cottonwood, willow, and spruce. No smoke of Indian village lifted above thickets. The tribesmen had moved to areas of less rigorous climate, east, south, or west, weeks before. The soaring peaks lifting their gleaming spires across the valley, their canyons deep-shadowed in blue gloom, stretched for miles to the north and south. Even his stout heart must have faltered, at least momentarily, at the grim barrier ahead.

Other than the Snake River Canyon, a route which he could hardly have anticipated from any vantage point, he would logically have selected Teton Pass as the most feasible crossing of the Teton Range to the southwest. Here the historians, at least those who accept the theory of a trans-Teton route, are in almost unanimous agreement, although some would have us believe that he made a frontal assault through Cascade Canyon. This hardly seems likely, since Colter, bold as he was, evidenced no characteristics of the foolhardy, and to his eyes the Cascade Canyon route could scarcely have appeared to offer a feasible crossing.

One cannot but puzzle a bit, however, as to his reason for crossing the range at all. From the broad valley of the Hole, the route northward up the Snake River into the Yellowstone was, to any eye, an easy one. The terrain sloped gently, there were no mountain walls to scale or circle and nothing to indicate any obstacle of consequence. Indeed, many notable historical scholars have opposed the Teton Pass theory, asserting that he did avoid the Tetons by moving northward. He would certainly have fulfilled Lisa's orders to contact nearby Indian tribes by the time he had reached Jackson Hole.

Accepting the Teton route, as we must in the light of later evidence, we add further stature to Colter's perseverance and venturesome spirit. He went over the mountains, perhaps because the Indians had described the route and country beyond to him, perhaps because he was seeking the reported "Spanish Settlements" on the headwaters of the Colorado River (Green River), or perhaps for the very simple reason that he wanted to see what was on the other side.

At any rate, the Idaho side of the range has given us the first really tangible clue as to Colter's whereabouts while on his winter journey. In 1930, about four miles east of the Idaho village of Tetonia, was found the "Colter Stone."

In the spring of that year, while plowing virgin land on his father's homestead, William Richard Beard, then a boy of sixteen, unearthed the stone from its resting place about eighteen inches beneath the surface. His attention was first attracted by the shape of the rock. It had been roughly formed to resemble a human head, flattened, with the unmistakable outline of forehead, nose, lips, and chin. When the stone had been cleaned, it was found to have been crudely carved. One side bore the name "JOHN COLTER"; the other was inscribed with the almost illegible figures, "1808." [Illustration, page 95]

The slab of gray rhyolite lava, from which the stone was shaped, is soft and easily worked. It would have taken no great amount of labor to have accomplished the job. Perhaps it provided a means of passing time while Colter was blizzard-bound or merely loafing in camp, taking a well-earned respite from days of arduous travel.

Immediately after the stone was given to the National Park Service in 1933 by Mr. Aubrey C. Lyon who had acquired it from the Beards, a controversy developed as to its authenticity. The carving of stones and tree trunks by early trappers and explorers was a well-established practice; several such evidences of their passing have been found. There have been hoaxes revealed also, and there were those who refused to accept the Colter Stone as valid. The evidence, what little there was to investigate, was carefully analyzed. There was no duplicity remotely connected with the finding of the stone. The Beards had never heard of John Colter. It had rested at a depth of some several inches beneath the earth's surface. Certainly Colter would not have carved it and then buried it, so the accumulation of soil above the stone must have been the result of some years and the stone had weathered before burial. It could hardly have weathered after being covered by earth. In the final analysis, it seems most illogical that anyone mischievously inclined would have been sufficiently informed to perpetuate a hoax at such a remote spot. A prankster would have deposited his bogus relic in a place where he could reasonably expect its ready discovery. Else why bother?

Colter's route, from the discovery of "his" stone, appears to have led northward along the base of the western side of the Teton Range until he perceived the next comparatively easy route for a return toward the east. Recrossing the Tetons he struck the western shore of Yellowstone Lake, called "Lake Eustis" on William Clark's "Map of the West" published in 1814. Tracing the route outlined on this inaccurate map, historical scholars propound that he followed the Yellowstone River to a crossing near Tower Falls, up the Lamar River and Soda Butte Creek, and back across the Absaroka Range. By way then of Clark's Fork and Pryor's Fork, he made his way back to Manuel's Fort arriving early in 1808.

So ended a most remarkable tour of some 500 miles, most of it made during the winter months. Aside from the rigors of winter climate, foot travel on showshoes must have proved easier with underbrush buried beneath the snow than hiking in summer over the same route.

That Colter made the journey, that he did traverse in one way or another Jackson Hole and the Yellowstone Park area, has been challenged by few historians, though all concede that his exact route will forever be a matter for speculation. The unprovable can hardly be proven.

Though Colter has not been celebrated in history as have other famous "Mountain Men" of a few years later, notably Jim Bridger, Bill Sublette, Joe Meek, and Jedediah Smith, to name a few, he remained a notable figure among his fellows until 1810.

It was in the spring or summer of 1808, following his return to Lisa's post, that Colter had his first encounter with the Blackfeet. It was the custom of these fierce and warlike Indians to send war parties south and west on forays into the lands of their enemies, the Crows and other tribes. They were not, however, particularly hostile to the whites, at least at this time.

Colter had again been dispatched by Lisa to "drum up" trade with the Indians. While traveling with a large party of Flatheads and Crows, near the Three Forks of the Missouri, Colter's band was attacked by a Blackfoot war party. In the battle that ensued, Colter was wounded, the Blackfeet were driven off, and the crippled Colter eventually managed to make his way back to Manuel's Fort. The Blackfeet were enraged by the presence of a white man, however accidental it may have been, fighting on the side of their traditional enemies. Colter's participation was apparently the inspiration for the hostility of the Blackfeet toward the whites that followed, and, quite probably, their hatred of Colter himself, which led to his most famous adventure.

Every school boy has read accounts of Colter's famous "run." Early writers made much of it, and various versions have appeared in print, all essentially similar. Summarized briefly, the records indicate that Colter, in the company of one John Potts, returned again in 1808 to the Three Forks country. Again he and his companions had a "run in" with the Blackfeet. Surprised while setting their traps, Colter was taken prisoner. Potts made the mistake of resistance against overwhelming odds and was promptly riddled with arrows and bullets after shooting one of the Indians. Colter was disarmed, stripped, and then released by his captors with the indication that he was to go. He had moved away from the Indians only a little way when several young braves armed with lances started in pursuit. He began his run for the Jefferson River, five or six miles away.

It is unlikely that many men ever ran better; certainly few have run for higher stakes. After some miles Colter had outdistanced all save one of his pursuers, but his strength was failing. It appeared that his desperate effort had been in vain. He stopped in despair to face the oncoming Indian, and as the warrior lunged, Colter seized the lance, which broke in his hands. The Indian, off balance, fell, and Colter killed him with the blade of the weapon.

With only a mile remaining to the stream, he turned to run again and managed to reach the river ahead of his enemies.

Here the accounts vary. One has it that Colter plunged into the stream and swam underwater to a nearby beaver house in which he took refuge. The other, and probably more likely version says he swam to an island and hid beneath a mass of driftwood that had lodged against the shore.

Although the Indians searched for him for the remainder of the day, probing the tangled mass of drift with poles and lances, Colter, in his place of concealment, avoided detection. After nightfall he made his escape and began his trek of nearly 300 miles back to Lisa's post.

Without weapons or any other means of obtaining food, he managed to reach the fort several days later in the last stages of exhaustion, feet lacerated and torn by rocks and cactus spines, half-starved and barely alive.

Colter made two more trips into the area of the Three Forks. Both times he narrowly escaped death at the hands of the Blackfeet; several of his companions were killed.

In 1810 Colter came to the decision that he had had enough of the Blackfeet, narrow escapes, and the repeated loss of furs, traps, and equipment. He left the country, this time to return to civilization without deviation or delay. He settled on a little farm in Missouri, married, and lived for his remaining years.

Colter died in 1813, reportedly from jaundice. The legal notice of the final settlement of this estate placed its value at $229.41.

So ended, at an age of only 38 years, the career of one of America's greatest frontiersmen, a forerunner of the famous "Mountain Men." Nevertheless, what a lot of living and adventure Colter crammed into the short span of his seven years beyond the Missouri.

Colter's part in the early exploration of one of the most rugged sections of America will forever stand as an heroic achievement. He was the West's first great pathfinder, a fitting figure to set the pace for those who followed his lonely paths into the wildest areas of the Far Western frontier.   ❖

THE MOUNTAIN MEN IN JACKSON HOLE

by Merlin K. Potts

Mountain Man. The very term has an aura of romance, and the mountain man of the Fur Trade Era was a romantic character as he most frequently appears in the novels of the wild Far West. He also appears as an uncouth, illiterate, morally degenerate, lazy lout addicted to prolonged debauchery. Between this extreme and the fearless, hardy, resourceful wanderer of the lonely plains and mountain highlands, lies the true measure of these men of the mountains. Some were as bad as they were painted; many were as fine as history describes them. They were the products of their time, neither better nor worse, than any cross-section of the men of any time.

They were, nonetheless, unique even among the pioneers of their day. Their chosen land was far beyond the outposts of the settlements, their fellows were few, and they moved through the most remote sections of America, often alone, sometimes in the company of a handful of companions.

Mountain men were the first to explore the Far West beyond the Missouri, through the Rockies, across the Great American Desert, from the Southwest to Canada, and to the western sea. They came not as explorers; such intent probably never occurred to them. Their sole interest was in the quest for pelts, particularly the fine fur of the beaver. Beaver hats were the vogue during the period of the

Western Fur Trade, roughly 1800–40. Until this headpiece was supplanted by the silk hat, the trappers followed the fur, their trails crossing and recrossing virtually every area where beaver were to be taken. Some were independent trappers, and some were attached to various fur companies. To the organizers of the trade, the "businessmen" behind the enterprises, fell the financial rewards. The trappers, except in rare instances, barely made a living at their profession. Their rewards were, many times, an unmarked grave or broken health, a maimed and crippled body, or, if they survived to a ripe old age of perhaps sixty years, memories of a lifetime of adventure multiplied many times beyond the normal conception.

They were indeed a breed of men apart. It is in no way remarkable that their story is one of the most fascinating in our history. Bridger, Smith, Fitzpatrick, Carson, Meek, Sublette, Jackson: these are among the famous names engraved upon the face of the land, markers to the indomitable men who left behind these reminders of the days when the beaver was king of the furbearers.

"Jackson's Hole," the great, mountain-encircled valley lying at the east base of the Teton Range, was, as that excellent historian Mattes puts it so aptly, the "Crossroads of the Western Fur Trade." Trapper trails led into and out of the valley from all directions through the passes to the east, Two Ocean, Togwotee, and Union, along the Hoback River to the south, through Teton and Conant passes at either end of the great range to the west, and along the valley of the Snake and Lewis rivers northward into the Yellowstone Country. From John Colter's memorable trek in 1807–08 through 1840, there was much activity throughout the region. With the decline of the fur trade, the valley became once again, and for many years thereafter, a place of solitude unvisited, as far as history records, by white men.

The name of Jim Bridger is synonymous with mountain man. Few frontiersmen from the time of Daniel Boone have so captured the imagination or been so voluminously treated in western lore. Bridger has been celebrated as the greatest of them all, his true exploits tremendous, his fancied feats fantastic. There were others who shared his fame, but he was overshadowed by none, perhaps equaled by a very few.

Bridger was born in Richmond, Virginia, on March 17, 1804, his birthday antedating by less than two months the departure of Lewis and Clark on the first great western exploration. The family emigrated a few years later to St. Louis, and Jim and his younger sister were left in the care of an aunt when their mother and father died in 1816 and 1817. By the time he was fourteen, young Jim was supporting himself and his sister by operating a flatboat ferry, then he became an apprentice in the blacksmith's trade. This mundane life was not for him. There were too many exotic influences in the St. Louis of that time which had tremendous attraction for a teenaged youngster. Indians on their ponies jogged along the street; Mexican muleteers and colorful Spaniards off the Santa Fe Trail strolled through the town. There were boatmen, fur traders, and plainsmen with their tales of buffalo, Indian fights, Lisa, Colter, and Lewis and Clark. What boy could resist the lure of adventure which beckoned so importunately just beyond the skyline? Jim could not; he did not. Little sister was growing up, expenses were mounting, and there was a fortune to be made beyond the western horizon.

In March 1822, just after Jim had passed his eighteenth birthday, the St. Louis Missouri Republican carried the following notice:

> To Enterprising Young Men. The subscriber wishes to engage one hundred young men to ascend the Missouri River to its source, there to be employed for one, two or three years. For particulars inquire of Major Andrew Henry, near the lead mines in the county of Washington, who will ascend with, and command, the party; or of the subscriber near St. Louis.
>
> [Signed] William H. Ashley

No mention was made as to the employment for one, two, or three years, nor was it necessary! What else but the quest for fur! Young Jim signed on, and a month later he was on his way to the promised land, one of the "enterprising young men" of Henry's company, bound up the river by keelboat to become a trapper. He was in distinguished company among experienced frontiersmen, though many of the crew were raw recruits, as green as Jim himself. There were Sublette and Fitzpatrick, Davy Jackson and old Hugh Glass, the latter to figure prominently in Jim's introduction to the frontier.

The outfit lost their horses, which had been traveling overland with a party under General Ashley's command, to the Assiniboines, however, and as Ashley returned to St. Louis, the balance of the command "forted up" at the mouth of the Yellowstone that fall. This was "Fort Union." Thus Jim became a "Hivernant." He wintered in the mountains and was a greenhorn no longer. When spring came he was a Mountain Man.

With the breakup of the ice that spring, Major Henry promptly started on the spring hunt, intending to combine trapping with trading with the Indians. The party was jumped by Blackfeet at or near the Great Falls of the Missouri, and the Indians drove them into retreat. They made their way back to the fort, with four men killed and several wounded. Bridger had his first taste of Indian fighting. It was not a palatable one.

In the meantime, Ashley had not arrived at the fort, but some time after the return of Henry's party, Jedediah Smith (also recruited by Ashley in the spring of 1822) arrived with one companion and the most unwelcome news that the general's party had run into difficulty with the Arikaras and was in dire need of reinforcements. Henry, with about eighty of his men, including Bridger, returned with Smith to aid Ashley, arriving in time to achieve a doubtful and short-lived truce with the Indians with the help of Colonel Leavenworth and a force of soldiers, trappers, and friendly Sioux who had moved up from Fort Atkinson.

Major Henry and his men, having received their supplies from Ashley, set out at once for the fort on the Yellowstone, intending to again proceed from there into the wilderness in search of furs. Shortly after the Arikara fight, occurred an incident that was to have a pronounced and lasting influence on young Jim. The aforementioned Hugh Glass was a hunter for the party, an elderly, tough Pennsylvanian. On the occasion which led to this claim to fame as a victim of one of the most tragic "bear stories" ever related, he was ahead of the party on a hunt, when he was attacked and mauled by a she-grizzly. So severely was the old man mangled that his companions despaired of his life. Here was a knotty problem. He could not be moved; he could not be left alone. Yet the party wanted to get out of the hostile Indian country and go about the business of collecting furs as speedily as possible.

Major Henry decided that two men must remain with old Hugh until he died. No one wanted to stay, but the Major proposed that every man contribute a dollar as an inducement to those left behind with the old man. The men were more than willing to subscribe to the arrangement. Jim volunteered to stay, and another, Fitzgerald by name, reluctantly consented to remain also. So it was determined, and the Major and the rest of the party moved on.

Old Hugh clung tenaciously to life, while Jim and Fitzgerald sat and fretted, constantly in fear of discovery and attack by the hostile Arikaras. Fitzgerald found Indian sign on the third day. As far as he was concerned, that clinched it. They couldn't do the old man any good, and he was certain to "go under" anyway. In the meantime, they were in terrible danger. He finally persuaded Jim to leave the dying oldster, taking with them Glass's rifle, powder, knife, and all his "fixins," because it wouldn't be reasonable to show up without them. They wouldn't leave the things with a dead man, and their story to the major would have to be that Glass had died. The old fellow was barely conscious, and they slipped away, catching up to the rest of the party just before it reached the fort on the Yellowstone.

Jim was worried, and memories of the old man haunted him. Suppose he hadn't died! Imagine his dismay when a few weeks later Glass appeared in the trappers' camp. Jim expected death at the hands of the hunter. He probably felt that he deserved it, but Glass seemed to be most interested in the whereabouts of Fitzgerald, placing the blame on him.

Glass had an incredible story to tell. Realizing that he had been deserted, he determined to save himself, and crawling, hobbling, barely able to move at all, he started for Fort Kiowa, nearly 100 miles away. He made it, and as soon as possible, thereafter, he started upriver again to locate Henry's party. He wanted "Fitz." When he learned that Fitzgerald had left the major and gone downriver to Fort Atkinson, Glass went after him with the avowed intention of revenge. He found him but found also that he had joined the Army. The commanding officer at Fort Atkinson heard his story, persuaded him that shooting a soldier would be a serious matter, and compelled Fitzgerald to make good the old man's losses; thus the matter was ended, perhaps not to the complete satisfaction of the justly irate old hunter, but at least without bloodshed. Jim never forgot. The rest of his life the lesson remained with him, and his record of service to others and devotion to duty rather than self-interest is sufficient evidence that the lesson was well-learned.

Bridger's exploits in the years that followed were legion. In 1824 he explored the Bear River, discovering the Great Salt Lake which at that time he believed to be an arm of the Pacific. He advanced from a trapper in the employ of others to a partnership in the Rocky Mountain Fur Company with Fitzpatrick, Milton Sublette, Fraeb and Gervais, when in 1830 they bought out the company of Jedediah Smith, David Jackson, and Bill Sublette. He is best known for his services as a guide. As his knowledge of the Rockies increased with his years of wandering over the west, he repeatedly served as a scout for the Army, in which capacity he was invaluable as his knowledge of Indians and their ways was second to none. He guided many notable expeditions, one of them the Raynolds party, into Jackson Hole. It was said of him that he could brush clear a patch of earth and inscribe thereon with a twig an accurate and detailed map of any section of the Northern Rockies, depending only upon a photographic memory of the terrain.

Bridger visited Jackson Hole for the first time in 1825. With Thomas Fitzpatrick and thirty trappers, he followed Jedediah Smith's route of the previous year, by way of the Hoback River from the south. They passed through the Hole, going north along the Snake River into the Yellowstone. This was probably the first trapping venture with Jackson Hole as the center of operations. Mattes says, in *Jackson Hole, Crossroads of the Fur Trade, 1807–1840:*

> This was a notable occasion, for the full glory of the Tetons was then revealed for the first time to these two young fur trappers who were destined in later years to become famous as guides for the government explorers and the emigrant trains, and as scouts for the Indian-fighting armies.

Bridger's trails, and those of many others, crossed and recrossed the valley at the foot of the Tetons many times in the ensuing several years as they moved to and from the rendezvous sites on Bear River, the Green, Pierre's Hole, and the Wind. Through this period the Hole justified its designation as the "crossroads." Traffic was heavy, and upon at least one occasion following the Pierre's Hole rendezvous of 1832, two men (not with Bridger) were killed by the Blackfeet near the mouth of the Hoback. These men did not, for a time, attain even the "unmarked grave" reward. Their bones were discovered and buried the following August by men of the American Fur Company.

Bridger's fame as a Rocky Mountain guide was well established by 1859, when he was employed by Captain W.F. Raynolds of the Corps of Engineers of the U.S. Army to assist his expedition in the exploration of the Yellowstone and all its tributaries. The Raynolds expedition left St. Louis on May 28, 1859, and included about fifteen scientific men, one of whom was the later renowned Ferdinand V. Hayden. The expedition wintered on the Platte near the present site of Glenrock, Wyoming.

During the several months that Raynolds and his men were idling away the winter, Bridger's stories of the Yellowstone aroused in Raynolds an intense desire to see these wonders for himself, and he determined to do so. The party left the winter camp on May 6, 1860, and headed for the Wind River country, eventually reaching Union Pass, so named by Captain Raynolds because he thought it was near the geographic center of the continent, on May 31. Bridger and the captain reconnoitered to the north but found the route discovered by Bridger in previous years, Two Ocean Pass, blocked by snow too deep to negotiate. They were thus forced, to their profound regret, to continue on down the Gros Ventre entering Jackson Hole on June 11. So Raynolds was unable to verify Bridger's tales of the wonders of the Yellowstone, marvels that Jim was as anxious for him to see as the captain was to see them.

The Snake River was a raging torrent, but a boat was contrived of blankets and a lodge-skin of Bridger's stretched over a framework of poles. The animals were persuaded to swim the river, and the party eventually managed the crossing. One man was drowned, however, while trying to find a ford. Raynolds and his men left Jackson Hole by way of Teton Pass and proceeded north through Pierre's Hole.

Although Bridger was engaged as a guide for many subsequent explorations, including a survey of a more direct stage and freight route between Denver and Salt

Lake City, he did not come again to Jackson Hole. He made his last scout for the Army in 1868.

Bridger's name appears on landmarks and features throughout the Rockies. In Wyoming there is Bridger's Pass across the Continental Divide a short distance southwest of Rawlins; Fort Bridger, a small town on U.S.Highway 30 near the site of the Fort established by Bridger in 1843; the Bridger National Forest; and Bridger Lake near the southeastern corner of Yellowstone National Park, to name only a few.

Bridger's "home" was in the mountains he loved. He bought property near Kansas City, a small farm and a home in Westport, where various members of his family lived, but Jim spent little time there until his declining years. He had a large family and was survived by four children from his Indian wives. Jim didn't believe in the practice of plural marriage as many of the mountain men did. He was married three times successively to women of the Flathead, Ute, and Snake tribes. His third wife died in 1858. He was a good family man. His children were sent to school in the east except for one daughter, Mary Ann, who was placed in the Whitman Mission School at Waiilatpu, Oregon, and who died tragically in the Whitman Massacre of 1847.

Jim Bridger's yarns of the West have long been famous. He could supply facts when facts were needed, but he loved to embroider his facts into fanciful tales for the edification and delight of the "greenhorns," to some extent because his facts were sometimes doubted. One of his greatest stories concerned the petrified forest of the Yellowstone. According to Jim, not only the trees were "peetrified," but there were "peetrified birds asettin' on the peetrified limbs asingin' peetrified songs." One time he was riding through this section when he came to a sheer precipice. He was upon it so suddenly that he was unable to check his horse which walked off the cliff into space and proceeded on its way because even gravity had "peetrified."

Jim died on July 17, 1881. His last years were not pleasant. He had a goiter from which he suffered, rheumatic miseries plagued him, and his sight failed. By 1875 he was totally blind. As his old eyes grew dim, he longed for his mountains. He said a man could see so much farther in that country.

His old friend, General Grenville M. Dodge, had erected above his grave in

Mount Washington Cemetery in Kansas City, a memorial monument which bears the inscription:

> 1804—James Bridger—1881. Celebrated as a hunter, trapper, fur trader and guide. Discovered Great Salt Lake 1824, the South Pass 1827. Visited Yellowstone Lake and Geysers 1830. Founded Fort Bridger 1843. Opened Overland Route by Bridger's Pass to Great Salt Lake. Was a guide for U.S. exploring expeditions, Albert Sidney Johnston's army in 1857, and G.M. Dodge in U.P. surveys and Indian campaigns 1865–66.

Jedediah Strong Smith, a contemporary of Bridger's, was another of General Ashley's "enterprising young men" who came west with the general and Major Henry in 1822. He was one of the rawest of the green hands, yet was one of the first to attain stature. He was older than Bridger by five years, head of an Ashley party at the end of one year on the frontier, in two years a partner with the general, and in three, the senior partner of the fur trading company of Smith, Sublette, and Jackson.

To say that Smith was second only to Bridger in his prominence as a mountain man, to attempt to place any of the leaders among the trappers in any order of rank or importance, would be like trying to rate the military commanders of history. Each in his own rugged individualistic way moved toward his own destiny. Many would have risen to even greater fame than they achieved, had they not met with misfortune early in their careers. So, we may assume, it might have been with Smith. He was already a famous figure in the West at the time of his untimely death in 1831.

He was an unusual type of man to be a frontiersman. Most would have said it was unlikely that he would last long or rise to any prominence in the rough, brawling, blood-and-thunder ways of the West of that day. He did not smoke or chew tobacco, was never profane, and rarely drank any spirituous liquor. He was a profoundly religious man, always carried his Bible with him, and allowed nothing to shake or alter his religious beliefs. For his day he was also a well-educated man, and one of the few who kept a journal in which he recorded in some detail his experiences.

For all this divergence from the usual ways of his fellows, he was respected and admired, accepted by the other trappers, affectionately known as "Old Jed" or "Diah," and even upon occasion referred to as Mr. Smith. He was the first of the trapping fraternity to reach California overland from the Rockies, the first across the Sierras, and the first to reach Oregon by way of the West Coast.

When Henry had established his fort at the confluence of the Yellowstone and the Missouri in 1822, Smith was sent back to St. Louis to advise General Ashley of the needs of Henry and his men for the following year. Smith then accompanied Ashley west in the spring of 1823, and, as mentioned previously, was sent ahead to enlist Henry's aid when Ashley ran into trouble with the Arikaras. He again returned with the general to St. Louis, and in February, 1824, Ashley sent him out again with a party which traveled overland by pack train. On this occasion Smith and his party made the first crossing, east to west, of the famous South Pass at the head of the Sweetwater River, the pass which was to become the crossing of the Great Divide on the Oregon Trail. This pass had been used by the Astorians, traveling in the opposite direction in 1812. (General Dodge's memorial, crediting discovery of the pass to Bridger in 1827 was thus in error, although various routes were being "discovered" and "re-discovered" at intervals by individuals who had no knowledge that others had preceded them.) A new era in fur trade history was opened when Smith's party found the rich beaver fields at the head of Green River. As Smith and his contingent moved north from the Green, they entered Jackson Hole by way of the Hoback, passed through the valley, and crossed north of the Tetons by way of Conant Pass into Pierre's Hole (the Teton Basin). Thus Smith preceded Bridger into Jackson Hole by a year.

Although Smith became possibly the greatest of the trapper-explorers, at least with relation to the wide territory covered in the course of his journeys, he did not return to Jackson Hole. He was killed by Comanches only seven years later on the Santa Fe Trail. Crossing desert country with a wagon train, Smith was scouting ahead for water when he was slain. His remains were never found. The story of his death came to light when Mexican traders who dealt with the Comanches brought his pistols and rifle to Santa Fe.

William "Bill" Sublette and David E. Jackson became Smith's partners in the fur trade when they bought Ashley's interests in the business at the rendezvous near the Great Salt Lake in 1826. Both of these men had been among those who made up Ashley's 1822 expedition. Sublette at that time was twenty-four years of age, a Kentuckian whose family moved to Missouri in 1817. Jackson has remained throughout the years an enigma. Practically nothing is known of him before his advent into the fur trade, or following his activity as a mountain man.

Sublette was the entrepreneur of the trio. It was Bill who handled the outfitting, the business contracts, and the transportation of trade goods and furs. That the partnership was successful is indicated by their disposal of their interests to Bridger and his partners in 1830 for an overall sum involving some $16,000. Sublette and his partners were shrewd enough to anticipate the gradual dissolution of the fur trade which influenced their desire to get out of the business. It was Sublette's wagon caravan from St. Louis to the Popo Agie and return in 1830 that proved the Overland Trail could be used by wheeled vehicles. This was the caravan that pioneered the immigrants' route to Oregon. Sublette later returned to the West as a trader in partnership with Robert Campbell and built Fort William (later Fort Laramie) in 1834.

Sublette and Jackson first entered Jackson Hole in 1826 after the rendezvous of that year near the Great Salt Lake. They crossed the lower end of the valley on their way to Green River, while their new partner, Smith, was headed with another contingent of trappers southwest across the desert toward California.

The system of trading at annual summer "rendezvous," several of which have been previously mentioned, was inaugurated by Ashley in 1825. The rendezvous site of that year was on Henry's Fork of the Green River. By such a method, more flexible than the previously used "fixed fort" system, the trappers assembled at a previously determined place, conveniently located for the widely separated trapper bands. The trader brought his goods to the site where furs were exchanged for the trade goods. It was a time of celebration, frolic, and general carousal for all concerned. The rendezvous site can be likened to the hub of a wheel. The trails followed by the trappers as they came in from the spring hunt and departed for the fall hunt were the spokes. Thus, rendezvous sites were on the Green, Wind, Popo Agie rivers, at the Bear and Great Salt lakes, in Pierre's Hole, and finally at Fort Bonneville. Jackson Hole was never a rendezvous site because of the difficulty of access for the traders over the high mountain passes surrounding the valley.

There is no positive evidence of trapping activity in the valley in 1827–28, although it is quite probable that the Hole received its share of attention. In 1829, however, Sublette and Jackson joined forces again in Jackson Hole where, by previous arrangement, they were to meet "Diah." Smith did not appear, and the partners were greatly concerned by his absence. Tradition has it that Sublette named "Jackson's Hole" and "Jackson's Lake" in honor of his associate while they were encamped on the shore of the lake waiting for Smith. Smith was eventually located in Pierre's Hole by one of the Sublette–Jackson party, Joe Meek, and the partners were finally reunited there, Jackson and Sublette moving over via Teton Pass.

Throughout the period 1811–40, nearly every mountain man prominently connected with the fur trade visited Jackson Hole. It was an area greatly favored by Jackson, which undoubtedly accounts for Sublette's most appropriate name. Following Colter's discovery of the valley, it was traversed in 1811 by three employees of the St. Louis–Missouri Fur Company, John Hoback, Edward Robinson, and Jacob Reznor. These three, en route to St. Louis in the spring, encountered the Astorian expedition (John Jacob Astor's overland party of the American Fur Company) and agreed to guide the party, commanded by Wilson Price Hunt, over a part of the westward route. This group entered Jackson Hole that fall by way of the Hoback River, then went west over Teton Pass. Robert Stuart brought a returning band of Astorians back in the fall of 1812 following the same general way and discovering the "South Pass" as they moved eastward beyond the Green.

British interests took the initiative in the exploration of the fur country following the War of 1812 and a general, and temporary, decline of American interest. In 1819 Donald McKenzie of the Northwest Company brought a large party through Jackson Hole and on north into the Yellowstone.

The Americans again entered the picture with Smith's previously mentioned venture of 1824, and from that time forward the list of Jackson Hole visitors reads like a "Who's Who" of the western fur trade. There were James Beckwourth (with Sublette), all of Bridger's partners (Fitzpatrick, Milton, Sublette, Fraeb, and

Gervais), Nathaniel Wyeth, Captain Benjamin L. E. Bonneville, and probably on one occasion the redoubtable Kit Carson.

The era of the mountain man was brief. It is doubtful that the trappers, traders, and fur company men realized the significance of their exploits in the expansion westward of a new nation. Yet without their activities, the exploration of the western lands might have been long delayed and the claim of the United States to the Pacific Northwest much less secure.   ❖

THE DOANE EXPEDITION OF 1876-77

FORT ELLIS, MONTANA TERRITORY TO FORT HALL, IDAHO

by Merlin K. Potts

TELEGRAM

St. Paul, Minnesota
October 4, 1876

To the Commanding Officer
Fort Ellis, Montana Territory

Under authority received from the Lieut-General, 1st Lieut. G. C. Doane, 2d Cavalry is ordered to make exploration of Snake River from Yellowstone Lake to Columbia River. He will be furnished a mounted detail of one noncommissioned officer and five men of the 2d Cavalry. The pack animals, 60 days rations for party, and the necessary camp equipage. You will cause also a small boat to be built by the quartermaster for Lieut. Doane's use, under his directions. Lieut. Doane will send back his Detachment from mouth of Snake River to Fort Ellis, and will himself return to his post via San Francisco, California, remaining at the latter place long enough to make his report.

By command of Gen. Terry
[Signed] Edw. Smith
Capt. of A. D. C.

Headquarters, Fort Ellis Montana Territory
October 7, 1876

Special Orders ⎫
No. 142   ⎬   Extract
        ⎭

II. 1st Lieut G. C. Doane, 2d Cavalry is hereby relieved from duty at his post and will comply with telegraphic instructions from Headquarters, Department of Dakota, Saint Paul, Minn. Date Oct. 4th, 1876.

III. The following named enlisted men are hereby detailed for detached service mounted and will report to 1st. Lieut. G. C. Doane, 2d Cavalry for duty.

Sergeant, Fred Server, Company "G" 2d Cavalry
Private, F. R. Applegate, Company "G" 2d Cavalry
Private, Daniel Starr, Company "F" 2d Cavalry
Private, William White, Company "F" 2d Cavalry
Private, John B. Warren, Company "H" 2d Cavalry
Private, C. R. Davis, Company "L" 2d Cavalry
They will be furnished with sixty (60) days rations.

IV. The Post Quartermaster is hereby directed to furnish 1st Lieut. G. C. Doane, 2d Cavalry with pack animals, camp equipage and boat, necessary to enable him to carry out the telegraphic instructions from Headquarters, Department of Dakota, Saint Paul, Minn., dated October 4, 1876.

By order of Captain Ball
[Signed] Chas B. Schofield
2nd Lieut, 2nd Cavalry
Post Adjutant

    The foregoing orders initiated one of the most unusual and bizarre expeditions in the history of the West. Unusual because of the lack of judgment shown in selecting late fall and winter for the journey; bizarre in the impracticability, in fact the impossibility, of execution of the orders.

    Lieutenant Gustavus C. Doane, selected to lead the party, was without question as capable a leader as could have been chosen. Lieutenant Doane had been detailed, with five cavalrymen, to accompany General Henry D. Washburn, Nathaniel Pitt

Langford, and their party of 1870 on the memorable exploration of the area destined to become Yellowstone National Park two years later. His record of service with that expedition was exemplary; he had a firsthand knowledge of much of the country to be traversed, at least over the early stages of the route; he lacked neither courage nor aptitude; and he possessed the ability to observe, describe and record in detail the experiences and observations of the expedition.

Hiram Martin Chittenden, in the biographical notes appended to his book, *The Yellowstone National Park*, has given us, very briefly, an impression of the man and his background.

Lieutenant Doane was born in Illinois, May 29, 1840, and died in Bozeman, Montana, May 5, 1892. At the age of five he went with his parents, in wake of an ox team, to Oregon. In 1849 his family went to California at the outbreak of the gold excitement. He remained there ten years, in the meanwhile working his way through school. In 1862 he entered the Union service, went East with the California Hundred, and then joined a Massachusetts cavalry regiment. He was mustered out in 1865 as a First Lieutenant. He joined the Carpetbaggers and is said to have become the Mayor of Yazoo City, Mississippi. He was appointed Second Lieutenant in the Regular Army in 1868, and continued in the service until his death, attaining the rank of Captain.

Doane's whole career was actuated by a love of adventure. He had at various times planned a voyage to the Polar regions, or an expedition of discovery into Africa. But fate assigned him a middle ground, and he became prominently connected with the discovery of the upper Yellowstone country. His part in the Expedition of 1870 is second to none. He made the first official report [to the War Department] upon the wonders of the Yellowstone, and his fine descriptions have never been surpassed by any subsequent writer. Although suffering intense physical torture [from a felon on his thumb, finally lanced by Mr. Langford] during the greater portion of the trip, it did not extinguish in him the truly poetic ardor with which those strange phenomena seem to have inspired him. Dr. Hayden [Ferdinand V. Hayden, United States Geologist, Department of the Interior, 1871] says of this report: "I venture to state, as my opinion, that for graphic description and thrilling interest it has not been surpassed by any official report made to our government since the times of Lewis and Clark."

Doane's record, unpublished, of his heroic attempt to lead his party through the wilderness of the Yellowstone, southward through Jackson Hole, and down the

"Mad River" to the Columbia is no less graphic in its vividness, no less thrilling in its expression of the hazards and the wild beauty of the land. It is marked by his absolute determination, no matter what the odds, to carry out his orders.

The lieutenant, as his journal records, had previous notice that the expedition was to be ordered, and partial preparation had been made before the orders were received at Fort Ellis, near the present city of Bozeman, Montana. Ration boxes were prepared and a boat was built, possibly the first such "prefabricated" craft ever constructed. It was a double-ender, 22 feet long, 46 inches in the beam, 26 inches deep, and curved strongly fore and aft. "It was built entirely of inch plank, and put together with screws, then taken apart again and the lumber lashed in two equal bundles, like the side bars of a litter. The whole forming an easy load for two pack mules."

For shelter the party carried an "Indian Lodge," constructed of army wagon covers cut to the proper pattern and with a diameter of 14 feet. The shelter weighed "but thirty pounds and sheltered the entire party."

> On the evening of October 10th, all preparations were complete for an expedition never attempted before in the winter time, and never accomplished since. The enlisted force was of picked men selected for special qualifications. In addition to those enumerated in the previous order, Private Morgan Osborn "G" Troop, the carpenter who built the little boat, and John L. Ward of "L" Troop, a teamster and packer, were taken along to bring back extra mules and the wagon from whatever point might be selected enroute.

On October 11, the expedition moved out from Fort Ellis and south-eastward toward the valley of the Yellowstone, reached that stream the following day and thence up the "wild and winding" river toward the "Mammoth Springs." The wagon bearing supplies was drawn by eight mules, two others carried the boat material, and each man was mounted except the teamster; an extra horse was led for him. All went smoothly until the third day, when, not far from the northern boundary of the Park, the "wagon came to grief, an unruly wheeler failed to pull at the right time, and the heavy vehicle cramped and went over crushing a hind wheel and reducing the body to something resembling kindling wood."

As a result of this not unexpected mishap, the wagon was abandoned, the load, comparatively undamaged, was made into packs, and after a two-day delay to rest the animals and arrange the loads, the party proceeded. In his entry of October 16, Doane enumerates the equipment carried by his party.

> Our outfit was an arctic one, omitting the stereotyped religious literature. We had buffalo coats and moccasins, rubber boots and overshoes, heavy underclothing, and plenty of robes and blankets. The detachment carried carbines only. Pistols are worthless in the mountains. In fact they are worthless anywhere in the field. I carried a 12-pound Sharpes Buffalo Rifle, with globe sight on the stock and chambered for long range cartridges. Our provisions did not include pemmican, Biltongue, lime juice or any other of the orthodox food preparations, but consisted of plain American rations, with some added commissaries, and an abundance of tea and tobacco. Matches were packed on every animal, and each individual carried several boxes constantly. Each man had a good hunting knife, not the crossed hilted and murderous looking kind but a short one intended for cutting up game. Our cooking apparatus included two fry pans, two Dutch ovens, four camp kettles, and some mess pans. We had plenty of axes and each man carried a hatchet on his saddle. To put together the boat required only a saw, a screw driver and a Gimlet, and we had a sack of oakum, with which to calk the seams. Before starting, there had been no solemnities, but each man's personal outfit was complete, arranged with a view to meet all possible contingencies without delay. I had duplicate notebooks, one of which Sergeant Server carried and from his, the only one left, I take my notes for this report. Of instruments, I carried a prismatic compass, Aneroid Barometer, max and min thermometers, and a long tape measure. None of these were provided by a generous government, but all were purchased by myself—as usual in such cases.

On October 17, the party lost the first of the pack animals.

> The morning air broke chilly and the air filled with frosty mist. One mule, a queer slabsided one was down, paralyzed across the kidneys. Here was an emergency. It was unable to stand alone when lifted to its feet, and would starve to death in a few days if we left it. But one remedy was available and that was a severe one. We heated kettles of water and scalded the animal along the spine. The first kettleful brought him to his feet, without further assistance, and a few cups full from a second restored his nerves

enough so that he kicked vigorously at his kind physicians, and refused further treatment. He was fearfully scalded but restored, and returned to Fort Ellis next spring of his own volition, got entirely well and survived all of his comrades of the pack train several years.

A heavy snow storm began on the night of October 19. The party laid over on October 20, and on October 21 made an early start for Mount Washburn, camping on its upper slopes that night, to the great relief of the lieutenant.

> This was the highest point to be crossed [9,200 feet] and I was terribly uneasy lest we should find it [the gap] blocked with snow as a depth of 30 feet is not unusual in February. Beyond and at our feet now lay the Great Basin of the Yellowstone, with its dark forests, its open spaces all wintry white, and its steam columns shooting upward in every direction. It was like coming suddenly upon the confines of the unknown, so differently did the snow landscape appear in the summertime. To us it was an enchanted land, the portals of which had just been safely passed, and we struck the downward trail full of enthusiasm, reached the open basin of Chrystal Spring Creek, the lowest point in the Great Basin, and camped in snow two feet in depth. Distance 18 m. Elevation 7250 feet.

On October 23, the party reached Yellowstone Lake, camping at its outlet. En route that day Doane encountered a tremendous elk herd.

> Taking light loads and leaving a man with balance of the plunder to keep off the bears as these animals are affected with a childish curiosity in relation to government rations, I started in advance of the party on the Lake trail, and was riding along slowly with my eyes shaded when my horse shied violently, with a snort, and stood trembling. I jerked away the shade and saw that I had ridden close up to a herd of at least two thousand elk. They had been lying in the snow, and had all sprung up together, frightening my horse. In a minute the great herd was out of sight, crashing through the forest, the old bulls screaming their strange fog-horn cry. It was a magnificent sight as the bulls were in full growth of horns, and the calves all large enough to run freely with the herd. No game animal has the majestic presence of a bull elk when he is not frightened, and in herds they manuevre with a wonderful precision breaking by file at a long swinging trot and coming into line tight-left or front to gaze

at some object of apprehension with a celerity and absence of confusion truly remarkable. In chasing them on horseback the first effect is to break them into a gallop, when they move more slowly and soon tire. In deep snow, when the herd breaks the trail for the horse to follow in, there is no difficulty in catching them.

I remember a chase in the Yellowstone Valley one winter day when two of us killed seventeen elk in less than an hour. Two large wagon loads of meat. On this occasion I did not shoot, as we had a long march to make and it would have caused delay, but watched them 'til lost to view and rode on. This sign of abundant game was exceedingly favorable and gave a confidence which nothing else could have inspired.

For the following two days the expedition remained in camp on the shore of the lake preparing the outfit for double transportation by land and water, the pack animals and part of the men to follow the shoreline, the others to take the boat across the lake. The little boat was assembled, the seams pitched, and the "Teeps" erected for the first time, bough shelters having been used previously.

On October 24, the men worked until late in the night making equipment ready and

retired to rest feeling all was well so far. During the night the stock stampeded and ran in close to the camp fire. A strange, threatening voice was heard in the dense forest nearby, a noise I had never heard before. A loud roaring was repeated. Applegate gathered his belt and carbine and I the big rifle, and while the others quieted the stock we moved out in the direction from which the sound came. It receded as we advanced, and shortly, with a continued crashing the animal retreated out of hearing into the timber. We soon came upon its trail and I sent back for a lantern. It was an old bull moose. It had pawed up quite a space and barked a couple of young trees with its horns thus producing the crashing sound we had first noticed. In accounts of moose hunting, read previously, I had never seen it stated that a moose gave any call whatever. These in the Park have voices, unquestionably, and use them with the utmost freedom. Toward morning we were again roused by a flock of swans circling over us with their wild and splendid notes, harmonized to a glorious symphony. In the morning I shot and wounded a large wolverine but did not stop him, and Starr, while prowling along the river bank below camp, shot a goose and found a small plank canoe in which he proceeded to paddle out into the lake.

Doane's description of the moonlight night which followed is a classic example of his ability to portray, in words, a picture of the wilderness he loved so well.

> That evening, the moon was in full and rising high above the lake and mountain, its soft light bathed the splendid landscape in floods of silver. The mighty ranges of the great divide were sharply outlined in cold, gleaming white. Below their ragged summits dark green forest masses filled the spaces to the margin of the water. At intervals steam jets played along the shore and the deep valley of the Upper Yellowstone reached the farthest limit of vision in the foreground. On the left front appeared a group of ghastly hills of chalky lustre by the banks of Pelican Creek, and beyond there a winding valley constantly rising as it receded with glittering channels, from thermal springs threading its long, green slopes. On the right front loomed up the yellow flank of Mount Sheridan, seemingly ready to burst forth with sulphurous flames; and flooding the space between lay the glorious lake with its rippling moonlit waters, its long sand beaches and deeply indented shores, its rocky islands of splendid coloring, its cliffs and inlets, and its still lagoons. A picture indescribable, unequalled and alone. From the distant marshes on the newborn Yellowstone came the sound of fluttering cries of restless waterfowl. From the echoing forest beyond, the mountain lions screaming and moaning at intervals while we put the finishing touches on our little vessel. Starr and Applegate, both expert boatmen, paddled the little canoe far out on the sparkling waters and sang Crow Indian war songs, as the work went on. The horses and mules having stuffed themselves with luxuriant mountain grasses, came up and stood meditatively with their noses over the camp fires in thorough contentment. It was a night and a scene to be remembered—a touch of nature vibrating into infinity.

In this entry also, seated by the campfire in a wonderfully expansive mood of the utmost well-being, touched by the serene beauty of his surroundings, Doane takes occasion to describe the other members of his party, the "picked men selected for special qualifications."

> Of the men who composed my party, Sergeant Fred Server was a Philadelphian of good family—a wild boy—who had settled down to a splendid daring soldier, an expert horseman, a good shot, a man of perfect physique and iron constitution.

Private F. R. Applegate was a small, wiry Marylander, used to hard knocks, thoroughly at home anywhere, full of expedients and know all about managing small water craft.

Private Daniel Starr was a man of powerful voice and massive form, had served on a war vessel, could turn his hand to any work. A man of infinite jest and humor, and reckless beyond all conception. He was already a celebrity in Montana on account of his uproarious hilarity, daring, and wild adventures. He ran the first boat on the Yellowstone Lake in 1871, had piloted several parties through the Park, and was always a volunteer in anything which promised a new field and a basis of new stories of the most ludicrous and most exaggerated character.

Private William White was a quiet, solemn young fellow, useful in any service, full of romantic ideas, sober, reserved. A man of fearless disposition.

Private John B. Warren was an Englishman, very set in ideas, an older man than the others. A man of intelligence, a most indefatigable fisherman and an all round utility man.

Private C. B. Davis was a born cook. He lived for his stomach alone and knew how to prepare food for its pacification. He saw no value in anything that was not edible; talked, thought and dreamed of good things to eat, but came out strongly over a camp fire. With a dishcloth in one hand and "something dead" in the other, he smiled beamingly into the yawning interior of an open Dutch oven, and inhaled with unspeakable delight the fragrant aroma of a steaming coffee pot. The above formed the regular detail for the expedition.

The others, Private Morgan Osborn, a carpenter, was a careful, sober man, not used to the mountains, faithful and honest and therefore useful.

Private John L. Ward was a hardy, vigorous man, good on a trail, in a boat, or on a wheel mule, a packer and a woodsman.

They were all enthusiastic on the subject of the present expedition, and were reliable intrepid men.

The "little vessel" was launched on October 26. No champagne christening this, but she rode on an even keel and rose in fine style to the waves. Doane, Starr, Applegate, and Ward voyaged out to Stevenson's Island and returned. The next day the boat was carefully loaded, and it carried everything except the saddle outfits on the animals. A broken-down mule was left behind, and with a mule harnessed to a tow line and one man to steer the boat off shore, she was so pulled along the beach for some twelve miles. At a rocky promontory, the tow line was taken in and two men rowed the craft around the point. Coming close to shore a wave struck the "little vessel under the lee quarter, and swamped her instantly." The water was shallow and everything was saved, but camp was made at once, fifteen miles from the point of launching.

The rest of the afternoon and half the night was spent in keeping fires going to dry out the baggage. The following morning it was discovered that waves had knocked loose some of the caulking on the bottom of the boat. It was repaired with the remaining oakum and pitch. At this point, the lieutenant was "very uneasy on account of the snow in sight on the Continental Divide in front of us" so decided to leave Starr, Applegate, and Ward to complete repairs to the boat, while he and the others, with all the "property should push on, cross the divide, break a trail and return with mules and horses to the lake shore to meet the party with the boat."

Doane and his group accordingly struck through the forest for several miles on October 28, reached the lake shore again and followed it to the "lower end of the southwest arm where the foothills come on the shore. Skirted around to the east side past the great group of silicate springs [probably the West Thumb area] and camped at the foot of the Great Divide at the nearest point opposite Heart Lake."

The following morning the land party remained near camp "in hopes that the men with the boat might come" and spent their time examining the springs. "One crater cone still active stands in front of the main group, pouring a stream of boiling water in the cold surrounding lake. It is here that anglers catch the trout and cook them on the hook."

The boat failing to appear, Doane and his men started up the slope to the Divide in a "heavy and blinding snow storm" through a "tangled forest." The weather turned very cold, and travel was difficult up the slopes in snow some two feet in depth. On the top of the ridge it was necessary to stop and build a fire. The animals and men were "loaded with snow and ice." The party reached a "hot spring basin" a mile from Heart Lake long after dark, built a great fire of seasoned pines, and spent most of the night drying out.

Doane was not at all satisfied with the route he had followed, and on the following day, in clear weather, the party worked its way back to Yellowstone Lake by a route which proved to be much shorter. The boat not having arrived, a watchfire to serve as a beacon was built on a bluff on the lake shore. Doane's entry in the journal for October 30 indicates his concern for the fate of the voyageurs, Starr, Applegate, and Ward.

> That was the third day and I was consumed with anxiety. A cold, wintry blast was driving down the lake in a direction at right angles to their course. The waves were running high and on the opposite shore we could see the surf flying against the rocks, covering them with glittering masses of ice. It was growing colder every minute, and the night was intensely dark. A driving sleet began to fall. This was dangerous, as it adhered to whatever it touched. Our apprehensions were almost beyond endurance. I knew those men would start that night no matter what perils might be encountered. They had twenty miles to come, in an egg shell boat which had never been tried in rough water. Nothing could live in that icy flood half an hour, if cast overboard. The wind and cold were both increasing constantly. Hour after hour passed. I followed the beach a couple of miles, but finding no traces returned. The Sergeant went in the other direction with like results. We were standing together on the shore despairing when suddenly there was borne to us on the driving blast the sound of boisterous and double jointed profanity. The voice was Starr's and we knew that the daring, invincible men were safe and successful. We ran to meet them and helped them beach, and unload the few articles that the boat contained. The oars were coated an inch thick and the boat was half full of solid ice. When the three men came in front of the camp fire, they were a sight to behold. Their hair and beards were frozen to their caps and overcoats and they were sheeted with glistening ice from head to foot.

> The boat had nearly filled three different times, but Applegate, who steered, threw her bow to the waves and held her there while the others bailed her out. They found that she would not bear the cross sea, so they kept her head to the wind, and forced her to make leeway by pulling stronger on the opposite side and working the steering oar to correspond. Thus they battled with the storm hour after hour until they had drifted twenty miles and reached the other shore. We changed clothing with them and after giving them a warm supper made them go to bed at once. The rest of the night we put in drying their clothes, as they soundly slept.

On October 31, the boat was cleared of ice by chopping it out with axes. Hot ashes were thrown in to dry her out inside, and "slipper poles" were cut and fitted under her to serve as runners. Dragging side poles were also attached to fend her off standing trees in passing. Two mules were hitched to the boat in tandem to drag her, and although progress was slow because the boat frequently became wedged between trees, and the deep snow made travel very difficult for the mules, the Divide was crossed, and "at 9 o'clock at night we left her on the Pacific slope of the Rocky Mountains, and went on with the tired stock into camp."

On November 2, the extra men, Ward and Osborn, with their horses and the three poorest mules, were started back to Fort Ellis since they were no longer needed. They were to pick up the mules and property left at different points on the way, and after an arduous trip of several days, they reached Fort Ellis safely.

The lieutenant and his reduced party now had seven horses and four pack mules. In camp at Heart Lake it was necessary to make extensive repairs to the boat; the cold had "shrunken the boards and opened all the seams." She was finally in order and launched on Heart Lake on November 5. During this layover the party feasted on baked porcupine which "resembled in taste young pork with a faint flavor of pine."

The party moved across and around Heart Lake on November 6, the boat loaded with all the equipment, and the horses and mules taken along the western shore. It was necessary to drag the boat across the frozen lower section of the lake for some three miles to the outlet. There the volume of the stream was so small it would not float the craft, even unloaded, over the rocks of the stream bed. For the next several days the "little vessel," the men, and the animals took a beating from the stream, the weather, and the terribly hard going.

November 18th. Reached camp in the forenoon with all the calking melted out of the seams and all the ice thawed out of the interior of the boat by the floods of boiling water passed through in the river channel just above. Took her out of the water and put her on the stocks to be dried out and thoroughly repaired. Her bottom was a sight to behold. The green pine planks were literally shivered by pounding on the rocks. The tough stripping of the seams, two inches or more in thickness, was torn away. Two of the heaviest planks were worn through in the waist of the vessel, and three holes were found in her sides. The stern was so bruised and stove that we had to hew out a new one. We took out the seats, floor, and bulkheads, and this gave us lumber enough to put on a new bottom. Mended the holes with tin and leather. Recalked her, using candles and pitch mixed for the filling. Split young pines and put a heavy strip on each seam and made her stronger than ever. This occupied the 19th which was a stormy day, and the 20th, which was clear long enough to enable us to finish the boat. When it is remembered that the wood had to be dry before the pitch would adhere, and that we were obliged to keep a bed of coals under the boat constantly to effect this on ground saturated with snow water and with the snow falling most of the time, it can be realized that the labor was of the most fatiguing description. Half of the party worked while the others cared for the animals and slept. Warren here came out as an invaluable member of the party. He kept the camp full of trout and we fared sumptuously. The stream from Shoshone Lake is the true Snake River and not the one we are on. It is twice as large as this one, and should be mapped as the main stream.

From this point we feel sure of plenty of water and will start with a partial load in the boat. The strain on the animals has been terrible as they have had to double trip the route almost constantly, which means three times the distance of actual progress. We have had but little depth of snow, and this, while favorable in one sense, has been detrimental in another, as it has allowed the game to run high on the mountains, where we had not time to go. Had there been deeper snow, the water supply would have been greater, the game would have been forced down to the valleys, and we would not have been obliged to use the animals so constantly.

The problem was to get where the boat would carry the property and make distance before the animals gave out. Also to get to settlements before rations were exhausted. I knew we had the formidable "Mad River Canyon" of the old trappers between us and human habitations. With plenty of large game in range, this would have caused no uneasiness, but we were descending daily and leaving the game behind.

I spend many an hour over this problem studying all the chances, and endeavoring to be prepared to act instantly in any possible emergency that might arise.

The party resumed their travel on November 21, Doane, Starr, Applegate, and White in the boat, and Sergeant Server, Warren, and Davis with the animals. The boat was headed down the now powerful stream, Applegate steering, and Starr astride the bow. Starr and White were armed with "spike poles" to push her off rocks and guide her into deep channels.

All was lovely. Starr had just begun to sing one of his favorite missionary hymns, something about "the Gospel ship is sailing now," when the river made a sudden turn to the left with a boiling eddy, and the boat crashed head on against the overhanging wall of rock, smashing all the lodge poles and compelling the boisterous singer to turn a somersault backward to save himself from being instantly killed. The gallant little craft bore the shock without bursting, and we went down stream [stern] foremost a short distance onto a shelfing rock where an examination developed the fact that nothing was damaged excepting twenty-two fine lodge poles.

On November 23, nearing Jackson Lake, the valley of the Snake was opening before the party.

"Hundreds of otter were seen. These growled at us in passing from their holes in the bank, not being accustomed to boats. We shot several . . . . An hour later we ran out into Jackson's Lake, and passed the train just as a mule fell under a log across the trail, struggled a moment, and died. Camped on the lake shore three miles from the inlet."[1]

The following day both land and water parties progressed along the western shore of Jackson Lake, the train finding

terrible severe traveling, climbing over rocks and through tangled forests of pine, aspen, and other varieties of timber . . . . We were too near the mountains to get a full view, but above us rose the huge masses of glistening granites too steep to retain much snow . . . . On the opposite shore are extensive Beaver swamps, and great areas of marsh, now frozen.[2]

The trout bite well, and we have a good supply. Ate our last flour today. Starr cooked one of the fine otter killed the day before. The flesh was nice looking. It was very fat and tempting. Baked in a Dutch oven and fragrant with proper dressing we anticipated a feast, were helped bountifully and started with voracious appetites. The first mouthful went down, but did not remain. It came up without a struggle. Only

Starr could hold it. The taste was delicately fishy, and not revolting at all, but the human stomach is evidently not intended for use as an Otter trap. Like Banquo's ghost, "It will not down." We did not try Otter again.

November 25th. Laid over, giving the stock a rest and repaired boat. Warren kept us well supplied with trout, which were in fine condition. In the afternoon my attention was called to an object moving in the lake. It proved to be a deer, swimming from the large island across to the opposite shore of the little bay. We had just finished with the little boat, and catching up the big rifle, while the others pushed off, Starr and Applegate rowed [me] out to intercept the deer. It saw us coming and turning to the left reached the shore about three hundred yards away, where it stopped shivering on the bank. We stopped and let the boat settle to steadiness and I fired. The deer was badly hit, and stood still. I fired again, and it fell into the water dead. It was the first game we had killed for a long time and came in the nick of time. After dragging it into the boat we found the two bullet holes about three inches apart and the last one had gone through the heart of the animal.

When the gun was fired first, the whole party turned out along the shore thinking that an avalanche was coming, and the noise of the second discharge had not ceased when we landed with the game. It was an echo. We spent hours testing it afterward, and surely nothing on earth can equal it. The report of the big rifle was followed by a prolonged roar that seemed to eddy in the little bay in a vast volume of condensed thunder, then charged up the great channel in a hollow, deep growl giving consecutive reports which bounded from cliff to cliff and these re-echoed until far up the canyon came back a rattle of musketry as on a skirmish line, mingled with mournful waves of vibratory rumbling. These were succeeded by cracks and rustlings, and a moaning sigh which slowly receded and died away far up along the height. Time, one minute and 25 seconds. We tried our voices together, and the result was deafening and overwhelming. There were seven in the party, and we were answered back by a hoarse mob of voices in accumulating thousands from the great gorge, and these, a moment after retreating up the channel called to each other and back at us 'til the multiplied voices mingled in a harsh jargon of wierd and wild receding volume of sound, ending in a long moaning sigh and a rustling as of falling leaves among the gleaming spires far away above us.

I then tried Starr's tremendous voice alone, and had him call, "Oh, Joe!" with a prolonged rising inflection on the first and an equally prolonged falling inflection on the second word, repeating it at intervals of 30 seconds. Experience had taught us that this call could be heard more distinctly and farther in the mountains than any other practiced. The sound of his voice at the first call had not ceased when a hundred exact repititions were reflected to the little bay. Then a rush of hoarse exclamations followed up the gorge and the fusilade of calls on every rock and cliff answered. "Oh, Joe!" And these sounds echoed and re-echoed a thousand times reaching higher and higher along the mighty walls, 'til faint goblin whispers from the cold, icy shafts and the spectral hollows answered back in clicking notes and hisses, but distinctly always the words, "Oh, Joe!"

A full bank of music playing here would give such a concert as the world has never heard. There is a wierd, unearthly volume and distinctness to the echo here, and a chasing afar off and returning of the sounds, unequalled and simply indescribable. We named this inlet Spirit Bay. [probably Moran Bay]

The party continued along the lake shore, the usual mode of travel being three men in the boat, four with the animals on land. Doane's horse was abandoned on November 26. All of the men were violently ill from the deer meat, the lieutenant diagnosing the sickness as "cholera morbus." The party was forced to lay over most of two days, but reached the outlet of the lake on November 30, started down river, and camped two miles downstream from the Buffalo Fork on that date, the boat having made about thirty miles that day.

December 1st. Moved on down the river. Sergeant and myself still very weak. Camped opposite Gros Ventre Butte which is in the middle of the valley, and in front of Mount Hayden [earlier name for the Grand Teton] and its mighty canyon. [From this description this camp appears to have been opposite Blacktail Butte, in the vicinity of the present location of Moose.] During the day Warren and White followed a herd of Elk 'til dark, but did not get one. Light snow on the ground. Weather warm. At noon 65 degrees. Distance 12 m.

The boat now carries all the property as the animals can carry no more. The river is a fine broad stream but the current is that of a mountain torrent and channel divides so often that we counted over one hundred islands today. Occasionally therefore, we came to shoal water by getting in the wrong shute and had to lift her over. The bed of the stream is entirely of coarse gravel and boulders, mostly of granite, and the banks are low. Fishing good, but fresh fish is too thin a diet to subsist on alone. We have now no coffee, sugar, tea, bacon, and worst of all, no tobacco. Nothing but a few beans left. The game is scarce and shy. I cannot hunt and keep the observations at the same time. The boat can now go faster than the stock, but we cannot separate with "Mad River Canyon" in front of us.

A glorious night, moon in the full, but empty stomachs. We are now far enough away from the lakes to be clear of the clouds of vapor and local snow storms. Our camp is about at a central point with reference to obtaining a view of the Tetons, and at a distance of fifteen miles from the nearest part of the range. [Distance actually about seven miles. Doane's estimate inaccurate.] The moonlight view was one of unspeakable grandeur. There are twenty-two summits in the line, all of them mighty mountains, with the gleaming spire of Mount Hayden rising in a pinnacle above all. The whole range is of naked rock in vast glittering masses, mostly coarse granites, but with some carboniferous and metamorphose rocks, the splendid colorings of these sheeted as they were with ice, contrasted finely with the snowy masses in all places where the snow would lie, and with the sombre depths of the great avalanche channels and mighty canyons. Of the latter the grandest is the Teton [Cascade Canyon] which half surrounds Mount Hayden, is four thousand feet deep, where it opens out into the valley in front of us, has a splendid torrent of roaring cascades in its channel and a baby glacier still at its head. The wide valley in front, seamed with rocky channels and heaped with moraines, is a grim ruinous landscape. There are no foothills to the Tetons. They rise on the glacial debris and in parks behind the curves of the lower slopes, but the general field of vision is glittering, glaciated rock. The soft light floods the great expanse of the valley, the winding silvery river and the resplendent, deeply carved mountain walls. The vast masses of Neve on the upper ledges from their lofty resting places shine coldly down, and stray masses of clouds, white and fleecy, cast deep shadows over land and terrace, forest and stream. And later on when the moon had gone down in exaggerated volume behind the glorified spire of the Grand Teton [Doane must have used the names Mount Hayden and Grand Teton interchangeably] the stars succeeded with their myriad sparkling lights, and these blazed up in setting on the sharpcut edges of the great, serrated wall like Indian signal fires in successive spectral flashes, rising and dying out by hundreds as the hours passed on. On the wide continent of North America there is no mountain group to compare in scenic splendor with the Great Tetons. There was not a pound of food in camp. We ate the last beans for supper, before going out to make notes on the Teton view.

The weakened party again laid over on the following day. They hunted carefully but to no avail, since the horses were too weak to carry the riders far afield from the camp, and the game was well up in the hills to the east. Warren, that "most indefatigable fisherman," caught sixteen magnificent trout, all of which were eaten for supper. Warren's horse was shot for food since it was the weakest and poorest of the lot.

He had not a particle of fat on his carcass, and we had no salt or other seasoning. Drew the powder from a package of cartridges and used it. We had been using the same old coffee and tea grounds for two weeks and the decoctions derived therefrom had no power in them, no momentum. For tobacco we had smoked larb, red willow, and rosebush bark. All these gave a mockery and a delusion to our ceaseless cravings. We chewed pine gum continually, which helped a little. We boned a quarter of the old horse, and boiled the meat nearly all night, cracking the bones as well, and endeavoring to extract a show of grease therefrom out of which to upholster a delicious and winsome gravy. The meat cooked to a watery, spongy texture, but the gravy sauce was a dead failure. Horse meat may be very fine eating when smothered with French sauces, but the worn out U. S. Cavalry plug was never intended for food. The flesh tastes exactly as the perspiration of the animal smells. It is in addition tough and coarse grained. We ate it ravenously, stopping to rest occasionally our weary jaws. It went down and stayed, but did not taste good. Weather turned colder toward morning. River running ice in cakes which screamed and crashed continually through the night.

For the next several days the party continued without serious mishap other than damage to the boat on two occasions when she crashed into submerged boulders. Warren continued to take trout successfully, the fish and horsemeat making up the sketchy bill of fare. On December 7, moving through the open country of the southern part of Jackson Hole, Sergeant Server and Davis, while hunting, found the cabin of a trapper, John Pierce. The old man was greatly surprised to see anyone with animals in the upper Snake River Basin at that time of the year and gave the men a substantial meal and some salt

which improved our regal fare by somewhat smothering the sour perspiration taste of the old horse. He also sent word to me about the settlement below "Mad River Canyon." River too shallow for fishing, but we had salt on our horse for supper.

December 8th. The old trapper came to our camp before we started, bringing on his shoulder a quarter of fat elk, also a little flour. He was a gigantic, rawboned, and grisled old volunteer soldier. We gave him in return some clothing of which he was in need and a belt full of cartridges, as he had a big rifle with the same sized chamber as mine. While talking with him, Starr and Davis were busy and soon we had a meal. The elk meat all went, the balance of the flour was reserved for gravies.

The old trapper gave me explicit and correct information about the settlements below. He was trapping for fine furs only, mink, martin, fisher, and otter. Said it would not pay to go after beaver unless one had pack animals and these could not winter in the valley.

He told me that he had not believed the Sergeant's story about the boat at first, and throughout his visit was evidently completely puzzled as to what motives could have induced us to attempt such a trip in such a way and at such a season. I sent him home on horseback with Sergeant Server, who told me after returning that he had been given another "Holy meal." Meantime we worked on down the river with renewed strength among rocks and tortuous channels. Worked until after dark and camped at the head of "Mad River Canyon." 15 miles.

The voyage down the Grand Canyon of the Snake, "Mad River Canyon," was a series of nightmares. Steadily deepening and narrowing, the canyon walls closing in with oppressive gloom, the river became almost completely unnavigable. It was necessary to handline the boat down boiling rapids, drag her over the ice of frozen pools, and portage the equipment, in this manner advancing six to seven miles a day. Doane writes that it was "very cold in the shaded chasm. Otter, fat and sleek, played around us on the ice and snarled at us from holes in the wall, all day long, safe from molestation in their fishy unpalatableness. We had no time to shoot for sport, nor transportation for pelts, and no desire for any game not edible. All day and as late at night as we could see to labor, we toiled to make six miles."

On December 11, Doane concluded to split his party.

No food left but a handful of flour. Shot White's horse, and feasted. It was now evident that we were not going to run the canyon with the boat, but must tug away slowly. We were about 42 miles from the first settlement, if our information was correct, but the canyon, if very crooked as it had been so far, might double that distance. I desired to get the boat through if we had to risk everything in order to do so. This canyon was the terrible obstacle and we were more than half way through it. Apparently the worst had been gone through with. All the men agreed to this with enthusiasm. We gathered together all the money in the possession of the party, and arranged for Sergeant Server, the most active and youngest of the party, and Warren, who could be of no assistance to those remaining, as his stomach had begun to give way, to go on next day with the two horses and one mule remaining and bring us back rations.

Sergeant Server and Warren loaded up as planned the following day, leaving the lieutenant and the other four men to continue with the boat.

The river was becoming better, the ice foot more uniform and the channel free from frozen pools when all of a sudden the boat touched the icy margin, turned under it, and the next instant was dancing end over end in the swift, bold current. All of the horse meat, all the property, arms, instruments and note books were in the roaring stream. A few hundred yards below there was a narrow place where the ice foot almost touched the middle of the river. We ran thither and caught whatever floated. The clothing bags, valise, bedding, bundles, and the lodge were saved. All else, excepting one hind quarter of the old horse, went to the bottom and was seen no more. All the rubber boots were gone excepting mine. The warm clothing all floated and was saved. We dragged in the boat by the tow line and pulled her out of the water and far up on a ledge of rock. 6 miles.

After this mishap, the Sergeant and Warren, who had been traveling along the river bank keeping in contact with the boat party, were sent at once on their way, while Doane and his men dried out and rested. The boatmen fought their way down the river for the next two days, but on December 14, the boat was hauled high on the bank in an apparently secure place. The last of the horse meat had been eaten for breakfast; no food was left.

The following morning the bedding was stored away in rolls with the valise, high up among the rocks, and Doane's party started, "unarmed, without food, and in an unknown wilderness to find settlements [previously described by the trapper, Pierce] seven miles up on a stream which we had no positive assurance of being able to recognize when we came to its mouth."

That day the men waded the Salt River (near the present site of Alpine) having spent seven days in the gloomy depths of the "Mad River Canyon."

On December 16, they were moving at the break of day in bitterly cold weather, and about noon reached an icebound creek which showed signs of placer washings. They assumed, correctly as it developed, that the settlements described by Pierce were on this tributary stream. Due to crusted snow they could make only about one mile an hour, but upon reaching the creek they walked on the ice and were thus able to make better progress. Some distance upstream the creek forked, and the men took the left-hand branch. By dark they had determined they were in error. They sheltered by a huge fire that night.

> We slept a little but only to dream of bountifully set tables loaded with viands, all of which were abounding in fats and oils. What conversation there was turned entirely to matters pertaining to food. Davis talked incessantly on such subjects, giving all the minutest details of preparing roast, gravies, meat pies, suet puddings, pork preparations, oil dressings, cream custards, and so on, until Starr finally choked him off with the Otter experience. None of us felt the pangs of hunger physically. Our stomachs were cold and numb. We suffered less than for two days before, but there was a mental appetite, more active than ever. It was an agony to sleep. All the party evidenced the same mental conditions excepting Davis who was hungry clear through, sleeping or waking. One feeling we had in common. It can be found explained in Eugene Sue's description of the Wandering Jew. We were impatient of rest, and all felt a constant impulse to "go on, go on," continually. The men did not seem to court slumber, and Starr had an inexhaustible fund of his most mirth provoking stories which he never tired of telling. We listened, laughed, and sang. Afterward we tried to catch a couple of Beaver which splashed within a few feet of us all night long. Had not a firearm in the party and here was the fattest of good meat almost under our hands, enough to have fed us for two days.

With the first gray streaks of dawn they were again on their way, working over the ridge to the other fork of the creek which they reached a few hours later.

A couple of miles farther on we stopped to build a fire and warm ourselves. Davis showed signs of undue restlessness. We had to call him back from climbing the hillsides several times. While we were gathering wood for the fire, I found a section of sawed off timber blocks such as they use for the bottoms of flumes. It had been recently cut on one side with an axe. This satisfied me without farther evidence that the mines above were not old placers, now deserted. The men were not so sanguine, but were cheerful, and we soon moved on again. In a couple of hours we came to an old flume. Shortly after, Applegate declared he smelled the smoke of burning pine. In half an hour more we reached a miner's cabin and were safe. We arrived at 8 p.m. having been 80 hours without food in a temperature from 10 degrees to 40 degrees below zero, and after previously enduring privations as before detailed. Two old miners occupied the cabin and they were both at home, having returned from a little town above with a fresh stock of provisions. They at once produced some dry bread and made tea, knowing well what to do. We had to force those things down. None of us felt hungry for anything but grease. About this time, to our unspeakable delight, Sergeant Server and Warren also arrived. They had passed the mouth of the creek on the 13th and gone below to the next stream which they had followed up fourteen miles without finding anything, and returning to meet us had found our trail and followed it, knowing that we had nothing to eat, while they had two horses and a mule with them. Mr. Bailey and his partner now gave us a bountiful supper of hot rolls, roast beef and other substantial fare, and we all ate heartily in spite of our previous resolutions not to do so. Cold, dry bread had no charms, but hot and fatty food roused our stomachs to a realization that the season of famine was over. The change affected us severely. I had an attack of inflammation of the stomach which lasted several hours. All of the men suffered more or less, excepting Starr who seemed to be unaffected.

The next day the party moved upstream to the little town, Keenan City, which consisted of a store, saloon, post office, blacksmith shop, stable, and "a lot of miners' cabins." Doane found that they had followed McCoy Creek, and that the settlements were collectively known as the Caribou mining district. The lieutenant records that his weight was down to 126 from a normal 190, and the others were similarly reduced.

A "jerky stage line" operated between Keenan City and the Eagle Rock Bridge on the Snake above Fort Hall, and Lieutenant Doane accordingly prepared the following telegram to be forwarded by the Post Adjutant at Fort Hall:

> Commanding Officer, Fort Ellis, Montana.
> Arrived here yesterday. All well. Write today. Send mail to Fort Hall.
> [Signed] Doane.

It was the lieutenant's plan at this time to construct small sleds for the rations and bedding rolls, these to be drawn by the two horses and the mule left to the expedition, and thus proceed downriver to Fort Hall. All was in readiness by December 23, and the party set out, proceeding some twenty miles through Christmas Day. While in camp on the evening of December 26, voices were heard in the river bottom nearby, where a party of troops had just gone into camp.

> It was Lieutenant Joseph Hall, 14th Infantry, with four men and a good little pack train. I shall never forget the puzzled expression on the face of this officer when he first met me. He conversed in monosyllables for a couple of minutes and then told us that he had been sent to arrest a party of deserters, half a dozen in number, which had been advertised for in the Montana papers, as having left Fort Ellis and were supposed to have gone through the Park and down Snake River. Thirty dollars each for apprehension and capture. The stage driver had read the papers it seems and denounced us to the Post Commander at Fort Hall. We first had a hearty laugh over the joke and he then placed himself and party at my disposal. We sat by the fire and talked nearly all night. (He was Post Adjutant at Fort Hall, and evidently knew something more than he felt at liberty to tell me, but he denounced Major Jas. S. Brisbin, 2d Cavalry, my Post Commander, in unmeasured terms, and told me that I was being made a victim of infamous treachery. This was a revelation but not a surprise.)[3]

Next day Sergeant Server and four men were sent with fresh animals to recover the boat and the bedding cached upriver. They returned the day following, reporting that it was only "fifteen miles by the trail on the other side of the river." They brought with them the equipment but not the boat, which had been crushed to splinters by an ice jam which had piled up in masses twenty feet high.

This was a bitter disappointment as they found the river open all the way down, and we so found it afterwards below. Here was another strange occurrence. In exploring as in hunting there is an element of chance which cannot be provided against. No foresight will avail, no calculations will detect, no energy will overcome. Caution might prevent, but with caution no results will be obtained. Risks must be taken, and there is such an element in human affairs as fortune, good or bad, I decided at once to make all possible speed to Fort Hall, there refit and returning bring lumber to rebuild the boat on the ground where it had been lost, and continue to Eagle Rock Bridge on the Snake River, previously going back far enough beyond Jackson's Lake to take a renewal of the system of triangulation and notes, lost in the river when the boat capsized. At Eagle Rock Bridge it would be necessary to rebuild the boat again in a different form and much larger, to run the heavy rapids of the lower rivers to Astoria, at the mouth of the great Columbia. The hardships and greater dangers we had already passed. With food for one day more we could have made the passage of "Mad River Canyon" despite the loss of all our weapons, instruments, and tools. We had run all the rapids but two, and these were easier than many others safely passed above. All the party enthusiastically endorsed this plan.

Lieutenant Doane was indeed a persevering and meticulously thorough individual, so much so that he not only planned to return to run the river from the point where he had been obliged to leave off but to retrace his route to a point above Jackson Lake in order to bring his notes to completion. It is difficult to follow his thinking when he indicates his intention of running the Columbia to Astoria, since his orders were to "make exploration of Snake River from Yellowstone Lake to Columbia River." His statement that the "greater dangers" had already been passed seems incompatible with the Hell's Canyon of the Snake below, a section of the river about which Doane must have had some knowledge. Here indeed were "risks to be taken" with "bad fortune" certain, quite probably occurring beyond a point of no return.

The party continued on December 29 toward Fort Hall, with Doane's journal describing in detail the route followed, the nature of the terrain, and the course of the river. They arrived at Fort Hall on January 4, having been met about half way between Fort Hall and the Eagle Rock Bridge by ambulances sent to bring them.

Captain Bainbridge, Commanding Officer at Fort Hall, "received us with the greatest kindness, and everything possible was done for the comfort of myself and party, by all at the post."

There followed an exchange of communications between the lieutenant and the Commanding Officer at Fort Ellis, Major Brisbin, with no reference therein to the charge of desertion. In the meantime, Doane records:

> We put in time at Fort Hall preparing to get together materials for another boat, intending to renew the expedition from 'Mad River Canyon.' Meantime I had made one of my Centenial Tents for Captain Bainbridge. While so engaged on the 8th of January, the following telegram came.
>
> Dated Chicago, Ill. January 6, 1877
> Received at Fort Hall, Idaho, January 8, 1877
>
> To Commanding Officer, Fort Hall, Idaho
>
> You will direct Lieut. Doane, Second Cavalry, with his escort to rejoin his proper station Fort Ellis, as soon as practicable. Acknowledge receipt.
>
> R. C. Drum
> A. A. G.

That Doane was very bitter at this turn of events is indicated by subsequent entries in his journal.

> This was the result. I simply note here an extract from Sergeant Server's journal. The only one left us when the boat capsized. "Lt. Doane was very mad in consequence of our having to return, and so were all the men, but we tried to make the best of it."
>
> Over a year afterward I received the key to this mystery. And here it is. It will be observed that there is some little truth in it, and much that is false. And bear in mind that my letter and telegram from Keenan City were received on the 28th December, and that I had not yet been heard from at Eagle Rock or Fort Hall.

TELEGRAM   Fort Ellis, January 2, 1877
To Assistant Adjutant General
Saint Paul, Minn.

I hear Doane lost all his horses, seven and mules, three, his boat and camp equipage, even to blankets, lived three weeks on horse meat straight; the last three days, before reaching the settlement, his party being without food of any kind. I recommend that he be ordered to his post for duty with his company.

[Signed] Brisbin
Commanding Post

Accordingly Doane and four men were returned to Fort Ellis by stage, arriving on January 20. Sergeant Server and White, leaving Fort Hall on January 12 "with the expedition's baggage and the extra horse" arrived at Fort Ellis on February 2 bringing to a close the final stage of the exploration.

One last entry in Lieutenant Doane's journal is worthy of mention.

In December 1878, I was told by my commanding officer, Major Jas. S. Brisbin, that he had disapproved of the expedition from the beginning, and had worked to have me ordered back because I had not applied for the detail through him. I make no comment.

A careful study of the journal reveals statements that can be questioned in the light of later knowledge. The mellifluous descriptions, the references to "hundreds of otter," and some other observations, together with the general tone of the document, may to some readers appear overdrawn. It must be borne in mind, however, that the journal was obviously written some time after Doane's return to Fort Ellis, and from Server's notes, since the lieutenant's records had been lost when the boat capsized on December 12. Server's notes were probably sketchy at best; much of the writing then was done from memory. That the account is colored by some imagination and a desire to make a "good yarn" of it is probably true, but forgivable, particularly when one considers the usual tenor adopted by writers of that day.

However critical the reader's opinion may be, it cannot be denied that here is an odyssey which defies comparison with any other record of winter exploration of the region. It was fortunate, beyond any reasonable doubt, that Doane's expedition did not continue. That his party could have survived ultimate disaster in the Hell's Canyon of the Snake is incomprehensible. That Doane, stubborn and fearless as he was, would have been turned back by any terrors the river threw at him is equally so. Doane was an explorer in every sense of the word, and he was determined to overcome all obstacles. He was, in truth, a man "to ride the river with." ❖

THE STORY OF DEADMAN'S BAR

by Fritiof Fryxell

Jackson Hole, widely reputed to have been the favored retreat and rendezvous of cattle thieves, outlaws, and "bad men" in the early days, has long enjoyed the glamour which goes with a dark and sinful past, and this reputation has by no means been lost sight of by those who have been active in advertising the assets of this fascinating region. But when the dispassionate historian critically investigates the basis for this reputation, he is surprised to find so little evidence wherewith to justify it or to indicate that pioneer times in Jackson Hole were much different from those in other nearby frontier communities, and he is forced to conclude that the notoriety of Jackson Hole, like the rumor of Mark Twain's death, has been slightly exaggerated. Doubtless the geographic features of the valley have encouraged the popular belief, for from the standpoint of isolation and inaccessibility, Jackson Hole might well have been a paradise for the fugitive and lawless.

But in fairness to the old idea, which one is reluctant to abandon, it must be conceded that among the authentic narratives that have come down to us from pioneer times, there are one or two which hold their own with the choicest that wild west fiction has dared to offer, and these bolster up to some extent the rather faltering case for Jackson Hole's former exceptional badness. Such a narrative is the story of Deadman's Bar.

There are few residents of the Jackson Hole country who have not heard of the Deadman's Bar affair, a triple killing which took place in the summer of 1886 along the Snake River and which gave this section of the river the name of Deadman's Bar. It is the most grim narrative and the most celebrated in the pioneer history of the valley, and its details are sufficiently bloody to satisfy the most sanguinary tourist, thirsty for western thrills.

EMILE WOLFF'S NARRATIVE

When Colonel Ericsson, Mr. Owen, and the writer visited Emile Wolff on August 9, 1928, we found him stricken with the infirmities of old age and confined to what proved to be his deathbed. Nevertheless his senses were alert and his memory concerning the period in question keen and accurate. The account he gave checked in detail with one he had given Colonel Ericsson a year earlier, and his recollection of names and dates agreed in most cases with evidence obtained later from other sources. In his enfeebled condition, however, Wolff was so weakened by the telling of his story that the interview had perforce to be cut short and certain questions left unanswered. A few questions Wolff declined to answer with the statement that there were features of the affair he would like to forget if he could, and there were others he had never told anyone and never would. What he had told other men, he said, he would tell us.

Concerning himself Mr. Wolff stated that he was seventy-six years old and a German by blood and birth, having been born in 1854 in Luxembourg. He received an education along medical lines in the old country. When still a very young man, only sixteen, he emigrated to America, where he served for some years in the United States Army in the Far West, part of the time as a volunteer doctor. His first visit to the Jackson Hole region was in 1872 when he came to Teton Basin (Pierre's Hole) for a brief period. In 1878 while serving under Lieutenant Hall, he came into Jackson Hole, his detachment being sent to carry food to Lieutenant Doane's outfit, which had lost its supplies in the Snake River while engaged in a geological survey of the Jackson Hole area.[1]

In 1886, Wolff stated, he came to the region to stay, settling first in Teton Basin. It was in this year that the Deadman's Bar incident took place. The account of this affair which follows is pieced together from the facts given by Wolff; no information gained from other sources has been introduced, and there have been no changes made in the story other than the rearrangement of its details into historical order. The account as set forth has been verified by both Colonel Ericsson and Mr. Owen, who were present at its telling.

In the spring of 1886, four strangers came into Jackson Hole to take up placer mining along Snake River, whose gravels were reputed to be rich in gold. The new outfit had been organized in Montana and originally had consisted of three partners, Henry Welter, (T.H.) Tiggerman, and (August) Kellenberger—"the Germans" as they came to be called. Henry Welter, who had previously been a brewer in Montana, proved to be an old friend and schoolmate of Emile Wolff's from Luxembourg. Tiggerman was a gigantic fellow who had served on the King's Guard in Germany. He seemed to be something of a leader in the project, claiming—apparently on insecure grounds—that he knew where placer gold was to be obtained. August Kellenberger, also a brewer by trade, was a small man who had two fingers missing from his right hand. The trio of prospective miners had added a fourth man to the outfit, one John Tonnar by name, also a German, under promise of grub and a split in the cleanup.

The miners located near the center of Jackson Hole on the north bank of the Snake River where that river flows west for a short distance. They erected no cabins, according to Wolff, but lived in tents pitched in a clearing among the trees on the bar within a few hundred yards or so of the river. Occasional visits to the few ranchers then in this portion of the Territory brought them few acquaintances. Once they ran out of grub and crossed Teton Pass to Wolff's place to get supplies. Wolff recalled that they paid for their purchases with a $20 gold piece. They wanted a saw, and Wolff directed them to a neighbor who had one; this they borrowed, leaving $10 as security.

On the occasion of this visit they spoke of building a raft to use in crossing the Snake at their workings, and Wolff tried to dissuade them from the project, assuring them that they did not appreciate how dangerous the Snake could be when on the rise, but they laughed off his warnings with the statement that they had built and handled rafts before and knew their business.

Wolff learned little, until later, concerning the mutual relations of the four men on the bar, nor concerning what success, if any, they had in finding gold.

Late that summer when haying time was at hand in Teton Basin, Wolff was surprised to see a man approaching his cabin on foot. "Seeing any man, and especially one afoot, was a rare sight in those days," commented Wolff. It proved to be the miner, Tonnar, and he asked to be given work. Curious as to what was up between Tonnar and his partners, Wolff quizzed him but received only the rather unsatisfactory statement that Tonnar had left the three miners while they were making plans to raft the Snake in order to fetch a supply of meat for the camp.

With hay ready for cutting, Wolff was glad to hire Tonnar for work in the fields. For a month the two men slept together, and during this time Wolff noticed that Tonnar invariably wore his gun or had it within reach, but while he suspected that all was not right, he made no further investigation. Wolff retained a mental picture of Tonnar as being a small, dark-complexioned man of rather untrustworthy appearance and manner.

Once Tonnar instructed Wolff to investigate a certain hiding place in the cabin and he would find some valuables which he asked him to take care of. Wolff did so and claims that he found a silver watch and a purse containing $28.

Then one day late in August, a sheriff and posse came to the cabin and asked Wolff if he could furnish information concerning the whereabouts of the miner, Jack Tonnar (at the time Tonnar was absent, working in the fields.) Briefly the posse explained that Tonnar's three partners had been found dead, that Tonnar was believed guilty of their murder, and that the posse was commissioned to take him. Horrified to think that for a month he had sheltered and slept with such a desperate character, Wolff could only reply, "My God! Grab him while you can!" Tonnar was found on a haystack and captured before he could bring his gun into play.

From the posse Wolff learned that a party boating from Yellowstone Park down the Lewis and Snake Rivers, under the leadership of one Frye (Free), had stopped at the workings of the miners but had found them unoccupied. Just below the encampment, at the foot of a bluff where the Snake had cut into a gravel bank, they had come upon three bodies lying in the edge of the water, weighted down with stones. They had reported the gruesome find, and the arrest of Tonnar on Wolff's place resulted.

Wolff, Dr. W. A. Hocker (a surgeon from Evanston), and a couple of Wolff's neighbors from Teton Basin hurried to the scene of the killings, a place which has ever since been known as Deadman's Bar. They readily identified the bodies, Tiggerman by his size, and Kellenberger from the absence of two fingers on his right hand. They found that Kellenberger had been shot twice in the back, that Welter had an axe cut in the head, and that Tiggerman's head was crushed, presumably also with an axe. Wolff gave it as their conclusion that the three men must have been killed while asleep and that their bodies had been hauled up onto the "rim" and rolled down the gravel bluff into the river, where they had lodged in shallow water and subsequently been covered with rocks. Probably the water had fallen, more fully exposing the bodies so that they had been discovered by Frye's men.

Wolff and Hocker removed the heads of Welter and Tiggerman and cleaned the skulls, preserving them as evidence. Wolff denied that they buried the bodies but claimed that they threw them back in the edge of the water and covered them again with rocks.

Tonnar pleaded not guilty and was taken to Evanston, the county seat of Unita County (which then embraced the westernmost strip of Wyoming Territory), and here he was tried the following spring before Judge Samuel Corn. Wolff was called to testify at the trial, mentioning, among other things, the incident of the watch and the purse, both of which he was positive Tonnar had stolen from his murdered partners.

To the general surprise of Wolff, Judge Corn, and others present at the trial, Tonnar was acquitted by the jury, despite the certainty of his guilt. What subsequently became of him is not clear. Wolff was questioned on this point, and at first declined to speak, later, however, expressing the belief that Tonnar probably went back to the old country for fear that friends of Welter, Tiggerman and Kellenberger might take the law into their own hands since the jury had failed to convict him.

Concerning the question of motive for the killing, Wolff stated that he knew Tonnar and the three men quarreled. The original partners planned to turn Tonnar loose when his services were no longer needed in sluice digging, etc., minus his share in the cleanup. To discourage his persisting with their outfit they had beaten him up badly a few days prior to the murders, but instead of leaving, Tonnar had stayed at camp nursing his bruises and plans for revenge, finally carrying out the latter to the consummation already described. Wolff did not believe that robbery was a factor of much importance in instigating the crime.

*　　*　　*　　*　　*　　*　　*　　*

From parties who heard the trial, it appears that there were no eyewitnesses to the tragedy, save the defendant. Therefore, the prosecution was compelled to rely solely on circumstantial evidence. The theory of the attorneys for the defendant was that the three deceased persons were prospectors without funds, and that they represented to the defendant that they had discovered a valuable mining claim and induced him to put up considerable money to grubstake and furnish necessary funds to work the claim; that soon after these men were on their way to the Jackson Hole country they began to pick quarrels with the defendant; that on the day of the shooting one of the prospectors remained in camp with the defendant, and the other two went away to do some prospecting; and that the one who remained in camp picked a quarrel with the defendant, and the defendant was compelled to kill him in self-defense. It was recalled that after the verdict was rendered the defendant got out of town in a hurry, taking the first freight train; that Attorney Blake was the principal trial attorney for the defendant; that he afterwards stated he never got a cent for saving the neck of the defendant who had promised to send him some money as soon as he could earn it; and that he had never heard from him.

NOTE:

Dr. Fryxell and Colonel Ericsson, immediately following their interview with Mr. Wolff on August 9, 1928, investigated the site of "Deadman's Bar." They found unmistakable traces of the diggings, the camp, and the road constructed forty-two years before by the four prospectors.

Dr. Fryxell's study of the site cleared up any uncertainty as to the exact location of this historic spot, which was placed on the north side of the Snake River in the SW ¼ of Sec. 23, T44N, R115W.

The sluice ditch of the miners, though overgrown with brush and partially filled with gravel, was easily located. It tapped a beaver dam located just above the bar and followed along the base of the terrace, discharging into the Snake about a half mile from its source.

Numerous prospect pits were found on the bar. Some of them appeared more recent than those dug by Tonnar and the other "Germans," thus were probably the work of later prospectors.

Dr. Fryxell states: "All of the workings (1928) now observable speak graphically of the expenditure of much hard labor from which returns were never forthcoming."

This statement is significant and is borne out by an old sign, crudely lettered, which was reportedly found later in the vicinity:

Payin gold will never be found here
No matter how many men tries
There's some enough to begile one
Like paper does flies.

❖

THE AFFAIR AT
CUNNINGHAM'S RANCH

by Roald Fryxell

Close against the Idaho–Wyoming border, at the headwaters of the Snake River, lies the high, mountain-girt valley of Jackson Hole. Fiercely beautiful in setting and richly historic in background, Jackson Hole and the raw, jagged peaks of the Teton mountains to the west have captured popular imagination as has no other region in the Rockies. Jackson Hole has become a fabled outpost of the vanished Western frontier, the legendary "last stand of the outlaws." And of all the stories which have given rise to that picture perhaps none is more starkly simple than one which has become known as "The Affair at Cunningham's Ranch."[1]

As in the case of other frontier communities, the story of the early settlers in Jackson Hole is one of isolation and hardship. When winter closed in and cut off the valley from the nearest settlements across the mountains, life was a struggle for survival against the bitter cold and drifting snow. Occupied with the task of making a home in the face of tremendous odds, the homesteaders were solid, law-abiding citizens with little time for lawlessness, and less for violence. On the rare occasions when gunplay broke out between men in the valley, it was of a nature that could hardly appear heroic except through the romantic eyes of a novelist. In the harsh light of reality, violence was brutal and ugly and dispatched with a speed and finality grimly typical of the frontier.

The Cunningham Ranch affair broke with a suddenness that shocked the entire valley. It was as cold-blooded as it was simple. A posse came riding in from Montana in the spring of 1893, and at a little cabin near Spread Creek, two men were cornered and shot for horse stealing.

Little news of the Spread Creek incident ever leaked out of the valley in the early days, and when the first general flow of tourist travel into Jackson Hole began nearly forty years later, the affair at Cunningham's Ranch was still a widely known, but reticently guarded story. By then most of the old-timers who had been members of the posse were dead, and those who were left still were not interested in discussing the matter. And so the story of the killing relies almost entirely on the memory and information of the one man who cared to talk about it, Pierce Cunningham.

A quiet, weather-beaten little man, Pierce Cunningham came into Jackson Hole with the first influx of settlers during the late 1880s and early 1890s. He homesteaded in the valley, and there, on Flat Creek, he worked his ranch and married and raised his family.

In the fall of 1892, while he was haying on Flat Creek, Cunningham was approached by a neighbor named White who introduced two strangers, stating that they wished to buy hay for a bunch of horses they had with them. One of the men, named George Spenser, was about thirty and had come originally from Illinois; the other was an Oregon boy named Mike Burnett, much younger than Spenser but already rated a first class cattleman after having punched cattle for several years elsewhere in Wyoming. Cunningham sold them about fifteen tons of hay and incidentally arranged to let the men winter in his cabin near Spread Creek, about twenty-five miles to the north. Since Cunningham himself intended to remain at Flat Creek, he also arranged for his partner, a burly Swede named Jackson, to stay with them.

Rumor began spreading during the winter that the two men on Cunningham's place were fugitive horse thieves. Some of the rustlers' horses, it was said, belonged to a cattleman in Montana; a valley rancher had worked for him and recognized some of the brands. Before the snow was gone, Cunningham had taken it upon himself to snowshoe to Spread Creek, investigate conditions, and warn

Jackson to be on guard. Once there, his suspicions were confirmed. Cunningham spent several days with the men, went with them to search for their horses, and recognized certain stocks and changed brands that left no question in his mind as to their guilt. The die was cast, and although he could readily have warned the men of their danger, Cunningham returned home without doing so.

The next spring, however, he ordered Spenser and Burnett to leave, and they did; but unfortunately for them, they returned to look for some horses on the very day they should have been absent.

This was in April 1893. Across the mountains to the west a man from Montana was organizing a posse in the little Idaho settlement of Driggs. Somehow, possibly on a tip relayed from the Hole, he had got wind of the rustlers on Cunningham's place and was coming to get them. One of the valley homesteaders saw the posse leader there with a group of fifteen men on saddle horses, and a few days later they came riding over the pass from Teton Basin into Jackson Hole.

In the valley, the leader completed organization of the posse. Including him, there were four men from Montana, two from Idaho, and ten or twelve recruited in Jackson Hole. Asked to join the outfit, Cunningham refused, and stayed at Flat Creek. The posse elected a spokesman, and then started up the valley to the Spread Creek cabin—a group of sixteen men, all mounted and heavily armed.

Under cover of darkness, the posse approached the cabin, a low sod-roofed log building in dark silhouette against the night sky. Silently they surrounded it: six men in the shed about 150 yards northwest of the cabin, three taking cover behind the ridge about the same distance south of the cabin, and the rest presumably scattered at intermediate vantage points. And then they waited for dawn.

Inside the cabin the unsuspecting men were sleeping quietly: Spenser, the older man, sandy-haired and heavily built; Burnett, the cowpuncher, slender and dark; and of course, Swede Jackson, Cunningham's partner. The two rustlers intended to leave when it got light.

Early in the morning the dog, which was in the cabin with the men, began to bark shrilly, perhaps taking alarm at the scent of the posse. Spenser got up, dressed, buckled on his revolver, and went out to the corral.

The corral lay between the cabin and the shed, and after Spenser had entered it, one of the posse called to him to "throw 'em up." Instead Spenser drew with lightning speed and fired twice, one bullet passing between two logs and almost hitting the spokesman, the other nicking a log nearby. The posse returned fire and Spenser fell to the ground, propping himself up on one elbow and continuing to shoot until he collapsed.

Meanwhile Burnett had got up, slipped on his overalls and boots, and fastened on his revolver. Then he picked up his rifle in his right hand and came out of the cabin. As he stepped forth, one of the men behind the ridge fired at him. The bullet struck the point of a log next to the door, just in front of Burnett's eye. Burnett swept the splinters from his face with his right hand as he reached for his revolver with his left and fired lefthanded at the top of the gunman's hat, just visible over the ridge. The shot was perfect; the bullet tore away the hat and creased the man's scalp. He toppled over backwards.

Burnett then deliberately walked over to the corner of the cabin and stopped with rifle in hand, in full view of the entire posse, taunting them to come out and show themselves. From inside the cabin Jackson pleaded with him to come in or he would get it, too. Burnett finally turned, and as he did so, one of the members of the posse shot him. The bullet killed Burnett instantly, and he pitched forward toward the cabin, discharging his rifle as he fell.

Now only Jackson was left in the cabin. A big, bumbling man with a knack for trouble, Jackson had once before been taken by mistake for a horse thief and been scared almost to death; when he was now ordered to come out and surrender with his hands in the air, he did so immediately.

The work of the posse was done. Mike Burnett lay face down in the dirt at the corner of the cabin, the bullet from his last shot lodged in a log beside him; George Spenser, his six-shooter empty, was sprawled inside the corral with four charges of buckshot and four or five bullets in his body. They were buried in unmarked graves a few hundred yards southeast of the cabin on the south side of a draw.

No investigation was ever made, no trial held, and the matter was hushed up. As years went by the subject of the killing at Spread Creek became a touchy one, and most of the men directly involved preferred not to talk about it. Swede Jackson, apparently thoroughly shaken by the incident, left the valley and did not return. The affair at Cunningham's Ranch was a closed story.

What information the members of the posse did volunteer in later years was in justification of their actions. The posse leader was a Montana sheriff, they said, and he and his men had come from Evanston, Wyoming, with the "proper papers" and deputized the Jackson Hole men. According to them there had been no intention of killing—the two victims had been given a chance to surrender, and after the affair one of the men in the posse had gone to Evanston to report it to the police.

Those in the valley who had not been in on the posse were not so sure of the legality of the shooting. Cunningham said he thought the leader was not an officer and reiterated that the posse had been instructed not to arrest but to kill. He stated that two local men had previously been asked to dispose of the pair but had refused. When asked who raised the posse and investigated the killing, Cunningham laughed and said he could tell but preferred not to. Asked if he cared to state whether the move was local or not, he quickly said, "Oh no—it wasn't only local."

Cunningham himself was rumored to have warned the outlaws to be on guard, having returned from the Spread Creek ranch only a short time before the killing. The story easily gained credence, since Spenser had caught the posse completely by surprise when he armed himself and started directly for the corral and shed where the men were hidden. Cunningham denied "tipping them off," and Jackson later said it was unusual for the dog to bark as it did that morning. Spenser probably sensed from the dog's actions that something was amiss and so put on his gun before leaving the cabin, a precaution which Jackson said the men had never taken during the previous winter.

Cunningham seemed more favorably impressed by the behavior of the two horse thieves than by any heroism on the part of the posse, an attitude which was general in the valley. Members of the posse had little to say about it.

In 1928, several years before his death, Pierce Cunningham recounted the story of the killing at Spread Creek and ended by pointing out the spot where the rustlers were buried. With two timbers he marked the sage-covered plot, one corner of it crossed by the road then running past the cabin, where George Spenser and Mike Burnett had lain since their death in 1893.

Years later badgers threw out some of their bones into the sunlight. ❖

PROSPECTOR OF JACKSON HOLE

by Fritiof Fryxell

In the 1880s and 1890s, it was widely supposed that the Snake River gravels of Jackson Hole, in Wyoming, contained workable deposits of placer gold, and there were many who came to the region lured by such reports and a prospector's eternal optimism.

Color, indeed, could be struck almost anywhere along the river, but the gold of which it gave promise proved discouragingly scarce and elusive. None found what in fairness to the word could be called a fortune. Few found sufficient gold to maintain for any length of time even the most frugal living—and who can live more frugally than the itinerant prospector? So through these decades prospectors quietly came and sooner or later as quietly left, leaving no traces of their visit more substantial than the scattered prospect holes still to be seen along the bars of the Snake River. Even today a prospector occasionally finds his way into the valley, and, like a ghost out of the past, may be seen on some river bar patiently panning. Probably he, too, will drift on. It is apparent now that the wealth of Jackson Hole lies not in gold-bearing gravels, but in the matchless beauty of its snow-covered hills and the tonic qualities of its mountain air and streams.

But one prospector stayed. Mysterious in life, Uncle Jack Davis has become one of the most shadowy figures in the past of Jackson Hole, little more than a name except to those few still left of an older generation who knew him. He deserves to be remembered—deserves it because of his singular story, and because he has the distinction historically of having been the only confirmed prospector in Jackson Hole.

He was "Uncle" only by courtesy for he lived a lonely hermit until his death, and so far as is known he left no relatives. He first appeared in 1887 as one of the throng of miners drawn irresistibly into that maelstrom of the gold excitements, Virginia City, Montana. In a Virginia City saloon he became involved in a brawl and struck a man down, struck him too hard and killed him. Davis, it should be remarked, was a man of Herculean strength and at the time of this accident, he was drunk. Believing himself slated for the usual treatment prescribed by Montana justice at the time—quick trial and hanging—he fled the city.

Davis reappeared shortly after this in Jackson Hole, the resort of more than one man with a past, and in the most isolated corner of that isolated region he began life anew. At the south end of the Hole, a few miles down the Grand Canyon, he took out a claim on the south side of the Snake River near a little tributary known as Bailey Creek. There he built a log cabin, the humblest structure imaginable—one room, no windows, a single door hung on rawhide hinges. This primitive shack was Jack Davis's home for nearly a quarter of a century. True, more than two decades later he built himself a new cabin, but death knocked at the door of the old one before he could move.

Down in the bottom of this magnificent canyon which he had almost to himself, Davis plied his old trade of placer mining, putting in the usual crude system of sluice boxes and ditches. In addition, he cultivated a patch of ground which yielded vegetables sufficient for his own needs and for an occasional trade. The income from both sources was ridiculously small, but his needs were modest enough. Primarily he wished peace and seclusion, and these he found.

The Virginia City episode never ceased to trouble him. It made him a recluse for life. He lived alone, and limited his associates almost entirely to the few neighbors who, as the years passed, came to share his canyon or that of the nearby Hoback River. Trips to town were made only when necessary and were brief. On such occasions it was his practice to cross the Snake near his cabin and hike or snowshoe up the west side to the store at Menor's Ferry, fifty miles distant. Having made his purchases, he shouldered them and returned by the same route. In the course of his journey he saw and talked to few. He rarely went to Jackson, the only town in the region. He is said to have been a sober man, afraid of drink.

Davis's solitary habits sprang from a haunting fear of pursuit, not from dislike of companionship. The presence of a stranger in the region made him uneasy, and he did not rest until his mission was known, sometimes pressing a friend into service to ascertain a stranger's business. He rarely allowed his photograph to be taken. Apparently his fears had little foundation, for no one from "outside" ever came in after him. Very likely Virginia City soon forgot him.

Davis's past was known to only one or two of the most intimate of his neighbors. They kept it to themselves. Nor would it have mattered had this story been more generally known—not in Jackson Hole where such a distinction was by no means unique, and where a man was judged for what he was, not for what he had been or had done.

Though a strange recluse, he was a man to be admired and respected. Physically he was tall, broad, of magnificently erect carriage—a blue-eyed, full-bearded giant. Stories of his strength still enjoy currency. According to one of these, Uncle Jack once lifted a casting which on its shipping bill was credited with weighing 900 pounds—lifted it by slipping a loop of rope under it, passing the loop over his shoulders, and straightening his back. And it was well known that for all his solitary habits, Uncle Jack was as kind and generous as he was strong.

It seems as though for the remainder of his days Uncle Jack did penance for his one great mistake. He impressed one as trying hard to do the right thing by everyone and everything. Such was his love for birds and animals that he would go hungry rather than shoot them. To callers at his shack he explained the absence of meat from the table by a stock alibi so lame and transparent that it fooled no one: "He'd eat so much meat lately that he'd decided to lay off it for awhile." His unwillingness to kill turned him into a vegetarian—here in the midst of the best hunting country in America. A hermit, yet Uncle Jack was hardly lonely. In birds and beasts of the canyon he found a substitute for human companionship. The wild creatures about him soon ceased to be wild. His family of pets included: Lucy, a doe who lived with him for many years; Buster, her fawn, whom the coyotes finally killed; two cats—Pitchfork Tillman, named for a prominent political figure of the times, and Nick Wilson, much given to night life, so named after a prominent pioneer of the valley; and a number of tame squirrels and bluebirds, not to mention Dan, the old horse, and Calamity Jane, the inevitable prospector's burro, which had accompanied Jack in his flight to Jackson Hole where it finally died at the advanced age of forty years. Maintaining peace in such a family kept Uncle Jack from becoming lonely.

Al Austin, who for many years was forest ranger in this region, and who in time came to enjoy Uncle Jack's closest confidence, presents an unforgettable picture of the old man and his family. Dropping in at mealtime for a friendly call, Austin would find Uncle Jack in his cabin surrounded by his pets, each clamoring to be fed and each jealous of attention bestowed on any creature other than itself. If the bluebirds were favored, the squirrels chattered vociferously. Buster, if irritated, would justify his name by charging and upsetting the furniture. Add to this the audible impatience of Pitchfork Tillman and Nick Wilson. Lucy was ladylike but nevertheless insistent. To this motley circle Uncle Jack would hold forth in inimitable language, carrying on a running stream of conversation—scolding, lecturing, admonishing, or when discord became acute, threatening dire punishment if they did not mend their ways. It is hardly necessary to add that to Uncle Jack's awful threats and the vivid profanity, which it must be admitted, accompanied them, the members of the household remained serenely indifferent, and there is no record that any of the promised disasters ever fell on their furry heads.

Having no windows, Uncle Jack left his door open during the good weather. One spring, a pair of bluebirds flew through the open door into the shack and, having inspected the place and found it to their liking, built their nest behind a triangular fragment of mirror which Uncle Jack had stuck on the wall. Uncle Jack then cut down the door from its leather hinges and did not replace it until fall. Six successive summers the bluebirds returned to the cabin, and finding the door removed in anticipation of their coming, built their nest and raised their young behind Uncle Jack's mirror.

Nearby, Uncle Jack made a little graveyard for his pets as they left him one by one. It was lovingly cared for. In the course of the twenty-four years which he spent there, the burial ground came to contain many neat mounds—mounds of strangely different sizes. But Lucy, Pitchfork Tillman, and Dan outlived Uncle Jack.

He would not accept charity even during the last year or two of his life when he was nearly destitute. Neighbors had to resort to strategy to get him to accept help.

On his periodic trips up and down the canyon, Austin brought the mail to Davis and to Johnny Counts, who lived next to the north. Counts and Davis, too, occasionally exchanged visits. On March 14, 1911, Austin called at Counts's and, finding that nothing had been heard of from Uncle Jack for some time, snowshoed on down the canyon to see if all was well.

The old man lay in bed, delirious. The last date checked off on the wall calendar was February 11. Outside the cabin, elk had eaten all the hay, and the horse and Lucy were at the point of starvation. Austin stayed by his bedside for several days, then, finding it impossible to care for Uncle Jack decently in the dark old cabin, summoned Counts. Several days later they moved the old man six miles up the river, carrying him where they could, most of the way pulling him along in a boat from the shore. The old trail was one Jack himself had built many years before. In Counts's cabin, a week later, Uncle Jack died.

Austin made Uncle Jack's coffin from one of the old man's own sluice boxes. Together the two men carried Uncle Jack to the grave they had dug for him at Sulphur Springs, nearby in the canyon. A wooden headboard on which Ranger Austin carved the inscription, "A. L. Davis, Died March 25, 1911," marks the grave—there Uncle Jack sleeps alone.

In Davis's shack was found the "fortune" which placer mining had brought him—$12 in cash and about the same value in gold amalgam. ❖

R. HARMON

MOUNTAIN RIVER MEN

The Story of Menor's Ferry

by Frances Judge

"This ain't W. D. Menor talking; this is H. H. Menor talking, by God. Holy Savior, yes!"

Both Bill and Holiday carried a mouthful of oaths that spilled out whenever they spoke. They cursed their friends and neighbors, they cursed each other, and they cursed themselves. But to lighten this burden of words when women were around, Holiday would say before a sentence, in the middle of a sentence, or at the end of one, "Holy Savior, yes!" or "Holy Savior, no!"

Bill never bothered to lighten his profanity.

Yet, in spite of cursing, they were men of dignity.

Everyone in Jackson Hole knew Bill and Holiday Menor. They were as much a part of the country as the Snake River or the Teton mountains. The type of men they were brought them here.

Then, as now, Jackson Hole had a marked collection of people. They were unshackled, and they had color. Strength was intensified. Weakness was vivid. Bill and Holiday were plainspoken, strong-dyed individualists. They belonged here.

The Menor brothers came originally from Ohio. They were tall men. Bill, eleven years older than his brother, was thin and long-boned. His nose and sharp eyes were like an old eagle's. Holiday's long body sagged a little. He had a grizzled beard, long, shrewd nose, and amused gray eyes. He prospected in Montana before coming to Jackson Hole. "My partner's name was Mean, but I was Menor," he would say. He claimed to have made over one hundred and twenty thousand dollars in one prospect. When asked what happened to the money, he always said, "Wine, women and song." He talked of going off to Old Mexico prospecting, but he never went. There was too much living to be done on the banks of the Snake River.

Bill Menor, coming to this valley in 1892, settled on a homestead by squatter's right. He settled where the Snake River hauls toward the great mountains. He was first to homestead on the west bank of the Snake River under the Tetons. He built a low, log house among the cottonwoods on the shore of the river; collected a cow or two, a horse, and a few chickens; plowed up sage and made a field; planted a garden; built a blacksmith shop; and in time opened a small store where he sold a few groceries: a lot of Bull Durham, overalls, tin pans, fish hooks and odds and ends.

And he immediately constructed a ferry to ply the unreliable Snake. Before settling in the valley, he spent ten days with John Shive and John Cherry "on the Buffalo." At that time he considered establishing a ferry somewhere along the Buffalo, but after talking with Cherry and Shive, he decided on the Snake River. And his decision was wise and farsighted.

Many settlers cut timber on Bill's side of the river, so the ferry was welcome. There were times when it was the only crossing within a forty mile stretch up and down the river. Once in awhile there was no crossing at all, when the river was "in spate," and Bill refused to risk the ferry. At such a time people were forced to go up one side of the river to Moran, cross the toll bridge and travel down the other side—eighty miles to travel eight.

The ferry, a railed platform on pontoons, was carried directly across the river by the current, guided by ropes attached to an overhead cable. The cable was secured to a massive log—called a "dead man." The ferry was large enough to carry a four-horse team, provided the lead team was unhooked and led to the side of the wagon.

Bill Menor charged fifty cents for a team and twenty-five cents for a horse and rider. A foot passenger was carried free if a vehicle was crossing.

In those early days almost everyone who came to cross the ferry around mealtime was invited to eat. If the river was too high for safe crossing and the persons who wanted to cross were in no particular hurry, Bill would keep them two or three days, bedding them and feeding them generously until the waters subsided and charging them only the slim ferry fee. "When you see them rollers in the middle of the river, I won't cross," he would say, apologizing in his grouchy way for keeping people around.

Anyone who stayed with Bill had to be washed and combed and ready to leap at the table at twelve noon and six sharp. Early in the morning as soon as the fire was built, he yelled at them, saying, "Come on, get out of bed. Don't lay there until the flies blow you!" Nothing angered him more than to have someone late for a meal, unless it was to put a dish or a pan in the wrong place. Bill had a place for everything, and everything had to be in place. Once the Roy VanVlecks spent the night with Bill. They washed the morning dishes before ferrying over the river. Bill, leaning against the kitchen doorcasing, criticized and cursed because the frying pans shouldn't go here and the kettles shouldn't go there. Yet he did not offer to put them on their proper nails or even show where they belonged.

That was Bill, and his neighbors understood. He was a man boiled down to his primary colors.

Bill was generally accommodating, but if he were particularly out of humor and had a natural distaste for a person who came along after six in the evening, he would refuse to ferry him over the river or keep him for the night. He apparently got satisfaction out of being downright mean to a few individuals.

When the Snake is high, it is ferocious. It boils, seethes, growls, beats its breast, and carries with it everything it can reach.

Once it got Bill.

A huge uprooted tree swept against the ferry with such force that the ropes broke, and the boat was carried downstream taking Bill with it. After a quick trip, the ferry grounded on a submerged sandbar. Neighbors gathered and conferred and hurried about trying to rescue Bill. He stood on the ferry violently cursing the rescue crew and acting in general as though they alone were to blame for the high water and his predicament.

Holiday Menor came to Jackson Hole about 1905. He lived for a number of years with his brother, Bill. But the disposition of each was cut on the bias, and the two disagreed over a neighbor. So Holiday took up land on the east shore and built his houses directly across from brother, Bill, and let the river run between them. Like a great many individualists, Bill and Holiday considered strong hate a mark of character, so they did not speak to each other for two years. Nevertheless, they were proud of each other, and the name of one always cropped up in the conversation of the other, mixed well with curses. And each watched across the river for the other, to make sure all was right on the opposite shore.

One Christmas the brothers were invited to the Bar B C Ranch for dinner. It was Holiday's birthday. Neither knew the other was to be there. When each arrived he was given a strong drink of whiskey to insure amiability. The two brothers shook hands over the Christmas table. Ever after they were on speaking terms.

And sometimes they spoke too freely, shaking fists and cursing each other over the river. There was much gusto in their living.

Though Bill read hardly more than the daily paper that came to him, Holiday subscribed to a number of magazines. He read seven long months of the year and "talked it out" the other five. He argued politically with everyone, whether they would argue or not. "Now, mind you, I'm telling you, this ain't W. D. talking; this is H. H. Menor talking, by God." And for emphasis he would bang things with a stick of stove wood. Once he came down on the red hot stove with his bare fist, and for a short while, political views were unimportant.

Gradually the land was taken up by the homesteader, or government leaser, and, the Menors were surrounded with neighbors. Then, as now, persons living ten or fifteen miles away were considered close neighbors. Everybody in the valley knew everybody else, or at least knew stories about him. For Holiday to have a close neighbor other than Bill was intriguing. Mrs. Evelyn Dornan, a Pennsylvania woman, homesteaded on the east bank, and her buildings were only a quarter of a mile below Holiday's. She called him the Patriarch of the Ford, and he called her the Widow down the River.

To have Mrs. Dornan ask how he prepared some dish filled him with pride. He enjoyed giving away his recipes. He would say, "You take two handfuls of flour, that is, and a pinch of salt, that is . . ." All his recipes were generously seasoned with "that is's." He was an excellent cook and loved to have his friends eat with him.

But there was the rooster episode.

Bill had a beautiful barred Plymouth Rock rooster, a huge single-combed domestic fowl with graceful feathers in its tail, and pride in its walk. But Holiday's rooster had only two feathers in its tail, its body was completely bare, and it had no pride.

It was a sad sight.

The Widow down the River laughed every time she looked at Holiday's rooster and wanted to take a picture of it. But Holiday said, "No."

"Holy Savior, no! I don't want that rooster shown as an example of what is raised on my ranch."

Fearing Mrs. Doman would take a picture of the fowl, he killed it, cooked it, and invited her to eat it with him. He never once thought that the bird might have been defeathered by disease. Mrs. Doman ate rooster and pretended to enjoy it. She was an understanding neighbor.

Both Bill and Holiday raised excellent gardens. To be fairly safe against frost, they never planted until the snow melted up to a certain level in the Tetons. They raised many vegetables. Their cauliflowers were as big as footstools. They raised currants and raspberries galore and made jelly and jam. And they raised flowers. Holiday always had pansies on the north side of his buildings. He called them "tansies." He and Bill always gave freely of their vegetables, berries, and flowers.

During the wild berry season, Bill would charge "huckleberry rates" to the local people—fare one way only—when the berries were ripe along the ridges and around the lakes under the Tetons.

Holiday would can between fifty and sixty quarts of huckleberries during a season. And since he drank periodically, he made wine. At any rate that is what he called it. He would make it of berries, raisins, prunes, beets, plus whatever else was handy—and never wait for the mixture to mature.

It would knock his hat off.

At five one summer morning, neighbors stopped at Holiday's returning from a dance. They were cold. They needed a stimulant, but Holiday had no wine. He had drunk it all. So they drank a cocktail made of gin and huckleberry juice, half and half. After finishing their drinks, two young men in the party decided to go shoot a rabbit for breakfast. They did.

"We shot it right in the eye," one said, holding up what was left of the rabbit.

The hind parts were shot away, slick as a whistle.

That is what gin and wild huckleberry juice did to a rabbit. Holy Savior, yes! What might Holiday's wine have done to it?

Holiday enjoyed the summer visitors in Jackson Hole. Bill probably enjoyed them also, but they could not lift him from his natural state of grouchiness. Once, after looking over the miles of sage that covered the levels of land that rise from the river to the mountains, an eastern lady said to Bill, "Mr. Menor, what do you raise in this country?"

Bill, a dyed-in-the-wool bachelor, looked at her and said, "Hell and kids and plenty of both."

He enjoyed startling people.

And he apparently knew what the "outsider" thought of a Jackson Holer. In 1915 he made a trip to the World's Fair with his neighbors, Jim and Mary Budge. When they had boarded a San Francisco–bound train, after a strenuous trek out of Jackson Hole, both Jim and Bill felt in need of a long drink of whiskey. Entering the smoker with their concealed bottle, they found one other man there. They did not like his looks, and they felt no need of him. Bill walked up and looked down at him with his eagle stare. "Do you know where we're from?" he said. "JACKSON HOLE!"

The man made a quick escape.

Though Holiday was more jovial than Brother Bill, his neighbors steered clear of him when he was in the process of making lime. He made and sold lime to neighboring ranchers. Some of them whitewashed their houses inside and out with it. Holiday chinked his houses with it. He also used it as a cure-all for man and beast. When he made lime he had to keep a steady fire going for thirty-odd hours in the kiln just behind the house in the bank. During these hours he was not fit company for man or beast. But his neighbors accepted his limey disposition as a necessary part of the process. Holy Savior, yes. What of it?

When late fall brought bitter winds, heavy fogs, and snow, the ferry was beached for the winter. From then on, all teams had to ford the river. A little platform was hung from the river cable to accommodate foot passengers. It would hold three or four at one time. The passengers mounted the platform from a ladder and sat down. Bill released the car; with a quick swoosh it ran down the slack in the cable where it dipped within ten feet of the river. Then the frightened passengers would laboriously haul themselves up the relaxed cable to the opposite shore.

In later years, when travel became heavier, a winter bridge was flung across the main channel. Putting in the winter bridge was the responsibility of everyone, friend and enemy alike. When the time was ripe, word was sent to nearby ranchers. On this day of days all cars and wagons were stopped and the occupants asked to help with the construction. If they protested, Holiday would say, "Do you want to use the winter bridge? Well, then help put it in!"

Giving a hot meal to the crew that laid the winter bridge became traditional with Mrs. Doman. While they carried logs and hammered, she baked and fried and boiled.

To find a crew to lay the winter bridge was never very difficult, but to find a few who were willing to help remove it in the spring was a very different matter. The ferry was running full blast. No one needed the bridge. No one was enthusiastic. This was spring; time to plant and build and plan. No time to tear down. To get men to the river for this seemingly useless task was worse than trying to get a fresh cow on the ferry without her calf.

So it came to pass that one spring there was only Holiday and one other man to move the bridge pole by pole, nail by nail, oath by oath. As a result any log that looked too heavy for two men to lift was rolled into the river. "To hell with it," Holiday would say, and dust off his hands. "Holy Savior, yes!"

In 1918, Bill sold his ranch and the ferry. The new owners raised the prices. Soon after the ferry changed hands, a Jackson Holer came along on foot. Finding the fare doubled he leaped, fully dressed and full of anger, into the Snake River and swam across. The pilot stood on the ferry, cursing the swimmer and yelling that he hoped he would drown.

Bill sold because he had enough of high water and low water. He had enough of fog, rain, wind, snow, and sunshine on the Snake.

Yet he could not drag himself away. He hung around his house, and at twelve noon and six sharp he would pace what was no longer his floor and swear because the meal was not ready. Mrs. Doman, who was then boarding at the Menor place, would get him to the door and say, "Go on out, Bill. The meal will be good when you get it." But this was no longer home. At last he dragged himself away from the ranch, away from the valley. He moved to California.

In 1925 the Gros Ventre slide occurred which brought tourists flocking to Jackson Hole. The great rump of Sheep Mountain had dropped away, damming the Gros Ventre River and forming a lake four miles long. This landslide occurred directly across the valley from Menor's Ferry and brought the owners a landslide of business. But Bill had sold and left the country.

By 1927 a huge bridge spanned the Snake not far from the Menor houses, so the ferry was beached and, in time, dismantled. But before the bridge was completed, Holiday had sold his land and followed his brother to California.

Now they were old men.

Just before leaving the valley, Holiday bought a new suit and and a new hat. He stayed a few days in Jackson at the Crabtree Hotel. One night, while he was in town, the ladies of some organization were having a dinner in the Club House, the upper floor of a huge frame building. An outside stairway led up to the hall. Holiday happened along just as a woman stepped out on the stairway with a pan full of dishwater. She threw the water all over him. Holiday walked on to the hotel, wet and violently angry. After a string of oaths that would reach from one end of the Snake River to the other and all its tributaries, he said to Mrs. Crabtree, "A man gets dressed up once in seventeen years and a woman has to climb up above and throw dishwater all over him. Why couldn't it have been a minute earlier or a minute later? Hell!" And he stomped off to his room.

Shortly before Bill's death, Mrs. Doman found the two brothers in San Diego in a little hospital on Juniper Street. Bill was bedridden, but his mind was keen. He cursed the bed in which he lay and talked of Jackson Hole. A sympathetic nurse had pinned on the wall at the foot of his bed a crude oil painting of the Teton mountains.

Holiday was able to be up and about, but his mind had begun to fade. Mrs. Doman took him mahogany "tansies" like those he once grew. Knowing he would never see her again, he gave her a handkerchief with his initials in one corner: H. H. M.

She knew that never again would she hear him say, "Now mind you, I'm telling you. This ain't W. D. Menor talking; this is H. H. Menor talking, by God!"

The brothers died within a year of each other.

But living or dead, they belonged to Jackson Hole. They were vivid, strong-grained men.

Holiday's buildings are gone. But Bill's low, whitewashed house still stands.

And the mad Snake rolls by, and the shadow of the great mountains moves over sage and building and river.   ❖

NOTES

Chapter 3. The Doane Expedition of 1876—1877

1. Years later, a peak almost due west from this camp, at the head of Waterfalls Canyon, was named Doane Peak, in honor of the Lieutenant.

2. Prior to the construction of Jackson Lake Dam, completed in 1916, the natural water level was some thirty-nine feet below the present high water line.

3. Parenthetical statement crossed out in the original.

Chapter 4. The Story of Deadman's Bar

1. There is a discrepancy here, since Doane's report of this expedition indicates that Lieutenant Hall and Doane met some distance down the Snake River from Jackson Hole, in 1877.

Chapter 5. The Affair at Cunningham's Ranch

1. This narrative is based on detailed historical notes obtained by the author's father, Fritiof Fryxell, more than thirty years ago, in conversation with early settlers of Jackson Hole—including Pierce Cunningham himself—who were in a position to furnish reliable information concerning "The Affair at Cunningham's Ranch." In the recording of these notes and their use in preparing the present account, every effort was made to reconstruct the episode as accurately and fully as possible, except that the names of the posse were purposely omitted.

BIBLIOGRAPHY

Alter, J. Cecil. *James Bridger, Trapper, Frontiersman, Scout and Guide.* Salt Lake City: Shepard Book Company, 1925.

Beal, Merrill D. *The Story of Man in Yellowstone.* Caldwell, Idaho: The Caxton Printers, Ltd., 1949.

Chittenden, Hiram Martin. *A History of the American Fur Trade of the Far West.* Stanford, California: Academic Reprints, 1954.

Chittenden, Hiram Martin. *The Yellowstone National Park.* Saint Paul: J. E. Haynes, 1927.

Doane, G. C. *Expedition of 1876–1877.* 44 pp. typed from original manuscript. Library, Grand Teton National Park.

Harris, Burton, *John Colter, His Years in the Rockies.* New York: Charles Scribner's Sons, 1952.

Mattes, Merrill J. "Behind the Legend of Colter's Hell, the Early Exploration of Yellowstone National Park," *Mississippi Valley Historical Review.* (September 1949).

Mattes, Merrill J. "Jackson Hole, Crossroads of the Western Fur Trade, 1807–1840," *The Pacific Northwest Quarterly.* Volume 37 (April 1946) and Volume 39 (January 1948).

Morgan, Dale. *Jedediah Smith and the Opening of the West.* New York: Bobbs-Merrill Company, Inc., 1953.

Mumey, Nolie. *The Teton Mountains, Their History and Tradition.* Denver: The Artcraft Press, 1947.

Sullivan, Maurice S. *Jedediah Smith, Trader and Trailbreaker.* New York: Press of the Pioneers, Inc., 1936.

Sunder, John E. *Bill Sublette, Mountain Man.* Norman, Oklahoma: University of Oklahoma Press, 1959.

Vestal, Stanley. *Jim Bridger, Mountain Man.* New York: William Morrow and Company, 1946.

Vinton, Stallo. *John Colter, Discoverer of Yellowstone Park.* New York: Edward Eberstadt, 1926.

The "Colter Stone," with John Colter's name inscribed on one face and the barely legible date, 1808, on the other. Found near Tetonia, Idaho, in 1930, the stone is now in the possession of Grand Teton National Park. [The John Colter story, chapter 1]

GRAND TETON NATURAL HISTORY ASSOCIATION, a National Park Cooperating Association, is a not-for-profit corporation established to aid educational efforts in Grand Teton National Park. Cooperating Associations, established by Congress, are not federal agencies and are governed by a board of directors made up of individuals from the community. All publishing activities of the Association are coordinated with the ranger naturalist staff of Grand Teton National Park. For information on Association publications, please contact:

Grand Teton Natural History Association
Grand Teton National Park
P.O. Box 170
Moose, Wyoming 83012